Ian Carroll is a best selling author, with all of his book paperback and also on Kindle.

Ian is the author of the 'A-Z of Bloody Horror' books, titles – ***'Warning: Water May Contain Mermaids'***, ***'Antique Shop'***, ***'Clown in Aisle 3'*** *and* ***'Pensioner'***. Also the author of the horror books ***'My Name is Ishmael'***, ***'Demon Pirates Vs Vikings – Blackhorn's Revenge'***, ***'The Lover's Guide to Internet Dating'*** *and* ***'Valentines Day'***.

He is also the author of the music books –
'Lemmy: Memories of a Rock 'N' Roll Legend' – which was a #1 in the UK, USA, Canada, France and Germany – ***'Ronnie James Dio: Man on the Silver Mountain – Memories of a Rock 'N' Roll Icon'***, ***'Leonard Cohen: Just One More Hallelujah'***, ***'Music, Mud and Mayhem: The Official History of the Reading Festival'*** *and* ***'From Donington to Download: The History of Rock at Donington Park'***.

The First three Volumes of the ***'Fans Have Their Say...'*** series are also available which are:

'The Fans Have Their Say #1 KISS - We Wanted the Best and We Got the Best'.
'The Fans Have Their Say #2 AC/DC – Rock 'N' Roll From the Land Down Under'.
'The Fans Have Their Say #3 BLACK SABBATH – The Lords of Darkness'.
'The Fans Have Their Say #4 GUNS N' ROSES – Welcome to the Jungle'.

Ian also writes the history section for the Official Reading Festival music site in the UK and has attended the festival 31 times since 1983.

Ian lives with his wife Raine, two sons – Nathan & Josh and a jet-black witches cat called Rex - in Plymouth, Devon, UK.

www.iancarrollauthor.com
Facebook.com/iancarrollauthor (Various Book Pages as well)
ian@iancarrollauthor.com

ISBN-13:
978-1721769698

ISBN-10:
1721769692

The Last Picture House

Saving Plymouth's Last Original Cinema Building

Foreword

Plymouth has had a very rich history of cinemas and attendance over the many years during the cinema boom and beyond.

When I was young in the '60s, '70's and '80s, growing up in Plymouth, there was such a vast abundance of cinemas to choose from in and around the area, that you were certainly spoilt for choice. From large single screen cinemas, to three and five screen 'almost' multi-plex's and finally the worse for wear venues, always referred to as 'flea pits' and we had quite a few of them.

Of the local cinemas that I remember going to, or knowing of, as a child, there was –

The Belgrave at Mutley Plain – now a 'for sale' snooker hall.

Studio 7 / Plaza at Bretonside – mostly showing 'soft-core' porn films, such as '**Emmanuelle**', '**Rosie Dixon Night Nurse**' etc. now the Ghurka Restaurant and Plaza Snooker club.

The Odeon on Union Street – later the 'Warehouse' and now the home of 'God TV', currently being renovated – was one of the biggest single screen cinemas in the country, at the time.

The State in St Budeaux – showing all the latest releases, now derelict – for many years after being a cinema, it was the Victoria Snooker hall.

The Forum in Devonport – now a Mecca Bingo hall – opposite where the Ark Royal pub used to be, which has now sadly gone as well.

The Drake/Odeon – originally a single screen cinema, then a three screen and finally a five-screen cinema, then demolished and rebuilt as the Grosvenor Casino; the only remaining part of the old Drake cinema is the Golden Hind replica (Sir Francis Drake's ship) on the front of the building above the main entrance.

These were six of the cinemas from my youth that I remember and some that I regularly attended. I always remember looking in the Herald on a Friday to see what was showing and hoping that my parents or my grand parents would take me out for a film one afternoon or evening, back in those days it was a real 'treat' a trip to the cinema. But there is one in addition to these that is still standing and this book is backing the campaign and the petition to save this cinema from also being destroyed for new developments and being left to our memories.

Back in the early '70s the only way to see a new film was at the cinema. It was exceptionally rare for a film to appear on TV

before it had been 'on release' for at least six years, because most films would show at the cinema and then maybe a year later they would be back again for another showing. Disney films were rarely, if ever, on the television and the local cinemas were always crammed with them and James Bond 'double bills' were always extremely popular as well. Back in the days of 'double bills' you could either enter the cinema at the start of the first or the second film and many times I would stay to watch some films twice or sneak from screen to screen – this was very easy to do at the Drake when it was a three screen cinema and whilst at school, we would often spend seven hours at the cinema of a Saturday afternoon into the evening.
I also remember when going with my mother and my younger sister Ann, that she would make us Marmite sandwiches to take with us, smuggling them in, in her handbag.

My first memories of attending the ABC were from way back in 1974, forty-four years ago when it was still a one-screen cinema with a balcony and stalls sections. The foyer was similar to as it is now, with the entrance to the upstairs section exactly the same, but the box office was either side of the entrance to the stalls.

I remember going to the cinema, on an afternoon out, with my friend Christopher Glover, his sister Rachel and their mother Pat; I can even remember what we went to see – '**Where the Red Fern Grows**' with James Whitmore and Beverly Garland, a tale of a boy wanting a hunting dog in the Ozark Mountains in America during the 'Great Depression'. Although not as exciting as other films released that year – '**The Towering Inferno**', '**Earthquake**', '**The Texas Chainsaw Massacre**' and '**Blazing Saddles**' – most of which I'd have been too young to see - it was still a trip to the cinema and one when the ABC was still in it's prime.
We walked up the open staircase and took our seats in the balcony and although the film wasn't that entertaining to a nine year old, the whole awe and spectacle of being in one of the

most impressive and beautiful large screened cinemas in the Plymouth area has stuck with me to this day.

Move forward four years and the biggest film of the year became my favourite film of all time.
It was September '78 and the summer was nearly over, but there was still time left for some 'Summer Lovin'...
I remember going to the ABC and queuing for what seemed like an eternity to get in to see '**Grease**' and got to the front of the cinema to be told that the performance was now sold out!! Those were the days before Blu-Rays, before on demand TV channels, before DVD's and even before Videos, when '*EVERYONE*' went to the cinema if they wanted to catch the latest movies or have a night/afternoon out. But, we went back the very next day and queued earlier and got to see a film that has stayed with me ever since, just like the trips to the ABC/REEL.
The First that I remember going to see in the newly constructed Screen 3 was a 'double-bill' of the '**The Land That Time Forgot**' and '**At the Earth's Core**' – two classic sci-fi/fantasy films from the era. I think that around the same time, I also attended a Ray Harryhausen 'double-bill' of '**The Golden Voyage of Sinbad**' and '**Sinbad and the Eye of the Tiger**', both brilliant films that I still enjoy watching now.

Skip quickly forward another four years and I got in to see the John Carpenter remake of '**The Thing**' on a late night screening in Screen 1 – even though I was only 17!!
The excitement of getting in to see an 'X' before you hit 18 years of age was one of the ultimate thrills; I remember going to see 'X' films all the time at the Belgrave Cinema in Plymouth as well, but they were very lax on their admission policy and I regularly went with my friend who was only 16!!

Around the same time I also remember going to an all night horror movie festival at the ABC, I can't actually remember what we saw, but I've been informed since by a friend (Theo Christian in Gateshead) that one of them was the Hammer film '**Legend of the Seven Golden Vampires**' – the worlds first 'Kung Fu Horror Film' – great times.

I remember a 'one off' preview of the film '**Personal Services**' which starred Julie Walters and was the story of Cynthia Payne who was the infamous Brothel Madam who accepted 'luncheon vouchers' for sex payments on her premises. Cynthia was present during the screening and after the film was shown, she answered questions from the audience, which was quite amusing.

Also, around my late teens I remember going to a late night showing of '**The Rocky Horror Picture Show**' – it was absolutely packed and I could see this being a popular draw now, if we can in fact stop the developers from destroying our memories.

So, fast-forward to now. One of the last films that I saw in Screen 3 was the Keanu Reeves film '**John Wick: Chapter 2**' on a Saturday night in the smallest screen and it was quite busy, almost half full, which for a 'tea time' viewing was probably quite good. I've also been to see '**Rogue One**' recently too and that was in Screen 1 and was packed, not surprisingly for such an amazing film, in such a vast auditorium.

People need a cinema of this size, with tickets at this price, close to the bus routes, no need to drive and for those that don't drive, the ideal option for not having to travel to the Vue and then deciding how to get home from there afterwards, walking or taxi being the usual only choice for people without transport of their own.

Having worked previously as an auditor for cinemas in Devon and Cornwall, I have been to many 'community' cinemas.
I've reported on the Alexandra in Newton Abbot, the Regal in Redruth, the Plaza in Truro and the Royal in St. Ives – to name but a few - but none are a patch on the REEL/ABC/ROYAL

CINEMA – or loved so passionately by so many people in the local community.
With a bit of *TLC* – which has been recently taking place - and possibly some amendments to the layout, especially if/when the Bingo Hall does close, we could have one of the best 'community cinema/arts centres' in the southwest, just look at what Exeter has done with their Phoenix venue in the city centre, which is used for theatre, concerts, comedy, films and art exhibitions.

So, all sign the petition, add yourself to the Facebook pages and let's move forwards and save –

Plymouth's Last Picture House...

Ian Carroll

18th May 2018

Introduction

The Cinema

"The Royal Cinema opened on July 15th 1938, replacing the Theatre Royal which had stood on the site since 1813. It was designed by William Riddell Glen for Associated British Cinemas (ABC). The ABC chain had been founded in 1928 as part of British International Pictures by John Maxwell, and by 1937 was the second largest cinema chain in the world. Unlike it's competitors, this growth was accompanied by profits and annual dividends with no financial crises.

With 2,404 seats the Royal was unusually large for a provincial ABC, but the nearby Gaumont Palace at 2,300 seats and Regent at 3,250 seats also held large audiences, something which may reflect the sheer number of military personnel stationed in Plymouth in the 1930s. An Odeon planned for Union Street but never built would have had a capacity of 2,500.

Played at the opening by Wilfred Southworth, the Compton organ, regarded as one of the best ever fitted to a cinema became well known at the hands of Dudley Savage. He began at the end of 1938 at just 18 years old and remained the resident organist until 1976. Weekly BBC radiobroadcasts and album releases brought Dudley Savage and the 'Plymouth Sound' to a wide audience.

The Architect

William Riddell Glen, born in 1884 began designing cinemas in 1919 and became the in-house architect for the ABC chain in 1929. His contribution has been overlooked to some extent, with little mention of him in architectural literature compared with George Coles and Harry Weedon. However, it is Glen's skill in interior planning which has helped to keep the Royal open for so long, facilitating the subdivision of the building, which has helped it survive social changes.

The layout of all Glen cinemas was superb, with patrons moving forward from the entrance and pay boxes to their seats, rather than having to negotiate the passageways and winding staircases typical of 1930s cinemas. The spaces he created made his cinemas the most profitable part of the ABC circuit, and although all his interiors displayed the same skill, each was an individual design developed for its location. Glen's 1938 cinemas are regarded as among his best, with the Royal described by Eyles as 'Glen on top form'.

The War

Though all cinemas closed with the declaration of war on September 3rd 1939, they soon re-opened, and cinemas played an important role in entertaining and informing the nation. On March 20th 1941, the area around the cinema suffered massive damage with fire gutting the Royal Hotel and Assembly Rooms but the Royal only closed for a short period for repairs, probably thanks to its modern fireproof construction. Twyford, in his description of the Plymouth blitz, said that

'Those modern buildings like the Royal, Odeon and Gaumont, and the 'ever faithful' Palace Theatre, received only slight damage and were able to continue their full programs within a short time of the heavy raids in 1941'

By 1943 a third of the population went to the cinema at least once a week, even with a 9.30pm curfew in place to save fuel and rubber. The war years were a golden era for British cinema, both in popularity and creativity.

There were 1,635 million cinema admissions in the UK in the first year of peacetime, with ABC having 18% of that total. About a third of 7-10 year olds were going to Saturday morning film clubs that year, including the 'ABC Minors' - which had been revived in October 1945. At the time film clubs were criticised by educationalists as bad for children's development-showing content which was too violent, showing too many imports, and being generally rowdy, charges which seem to be leveled at the entertainment of every generation of children. Indeed, 'juvenile delinquency' was a term which had been coined during the war due to limited parental supervision.

The Postwar Challenge

Pearl and Dean first appeared on screens in February 1952 with advertising being introduced to offset the revenue lost to falling attendances and reduced ice-cream sales after the abolition of sweet rationing. Attendances continued to fall and by the end of the 1950s TV had taken over as mass entertainment, with cinemas began closing down in significant numbers, a trend which continued over the next 20 years. Live shows were introduced at many of the larger ABC's, as a way to bolster income and between 1954 and 1976 a wide variety of music and entertainment acts appeared at the ABC, including 2 appearances by the Beatles.

During the 1970s while the total number of cinemas fell in the UK the number of screens rose sharply as a result of twinning and tripling conversions. With the Forum Devonport (1938) having closed in 1960 and the State in St Budeaux (1939) shutting in 1973, The ABC and Drake were converted to multi-screen cinemas at a similar time in the mid 1970's, securing their future at least in the short term. After a final live performance by Morecambe and Wise in 1976, The Stalls at the ABC were converted into a Bingo hall, at first known as the EMI Social club and now Gala Bingo. The Circle became screens 1 & 2 and Screen 3 was inserted in the double height foyer. Nationally attendances continued to fall and by 1980 cinema attendance was at 2% of the 1950 figure. However the Drake Odeon and the ABC were both getting Saturday children's matinee attendances of 800 in 1979- 3% of the UK total and showing that the city didn't necessarily mirror national trends, something which may explain the survival of both the ABC and Drake throughout the 1980's.

The Theatre District

Following the severe damage inflicted during the war the reconstruction of the city, first proposed in the 1943 Plan for Plymouth, has been described as 'nationally exceptional and significant' by Professor Jeremy Gould. The Royal Cinema was one of the very few pre-war buildings specifically included in the Plan for Plymouth, forming the nucleus of a proposed theatre district.

It was originally intended to build a new hotel on the site of Foulston's Hotel and Assembly Rooms, and WR Glen had drawn up detailed plans for this. The hotel would have adjoined the cinema, which explains the 'unfinished' corner on the left of the building where the bingo hall entrance now sits. However, following the blitz the vacant site left by the destruction of the original hotel was filled with Nissen huts which formed a temporary NAAFI until the Hoe Centre on Notte Street could be built.

By the 1980's the theatre district proposed by Abercrombie was complete, with the new Theatre Royal, The ABC Cinema, the Athenaeum, Westward Television/TSW and the Drake Cinema all in place. The Royal Cinema, Derry's Cross and the Bank pub are the only reminders of the pre-war street layout, with the site of the old Royal Hotel now taken up by the Theatre Royal Car park and Princess Way. Sadly the theatre district has lost both Westward Television and the Drake Cinema, but the Royal Cinema, the Theatre Royal and the Athenaeum still entertain and educate.

What's In a Name

*The cinema opened as the '**Royal**' in 1938, reflecting the history of the site. Neon lighting was fitted to ABC's from 1949, along with a redesigned ABC logo. Due to the loss of so many venues in the blitz the cinema served as a theatre as well as showing films, with the name '**Theatre Royal**' added to the canopy. This was short lived though and by 1958, in line with other ABC cinemas, the name 'Royal' was dropped and new corporate '**ABC**' branding applied, along with a new canopy which is still above the entrance today. Warner Bothers had controlled the ABC chain since 1946, but sold their stake to EMI in 1969 and the '**EMI**' logo was added to the existing ABC signage.*

*From the 1980s onwards the British cinema industry went through a complex series of changes in ownership and branding. ABC became '**Cannon**' in 1987 when Thorn EMI Screen Entertainment sold up to businessman Alan Bond, who then sold the chain on a week later for a multimillion pound profit. Cannon was taken over by Pathe in the early 1990s with the '**MGM**' brand appearing on cinemas. Via a brief period* *under the ownership of Virgin the remains of the Odeon and ABC chains were merged and by 2000 the Odeon brand was applied to the remaining ABC's. However, a sole survivor, the Westover Bournemouth, remained an ABC until it's closure in January 2017. In Plymouth a management buyout had prevented the ingominy of Odeon branding, with the* ***'ABC'*** *name returning to the Royal in the mid 1990s. The current operator, Reel Cinemas, took over in 2006 and the cinema has been branded a* ***'Reel'*** *since then.*

The Last Picture House

"Seven cinemas in Plymouth and three in Devonport were lost in the blitz and after the war the only new cinema to be built was the Drake- intended as the first in a chain of Twentieth Century Fox cinemas. This plan foundered and soon the Drake became part of the Odeon circuit, resulting in 3 Odeon's in close proximity. The Regent (an Odeon since 1940) soon closed down and was demolished, then following the closure of the other Odeon (formerly the Gaumont Palace) in 1980, Plymouth city centre was left with the ABC and the Drake. Further afield the Plaza on Bretonside (built in 1934) had closed in 1981 after its twilight years as an adult cinema, and the Belgrave in Mutley shut its doors in 1983.

With the opening of the Vue multiplex to the east of the city centre, the Drake sadly closed in 1999 and was demolished, though 'the Ship' survives, marooned on the casino building which now stands on the site. Of the pre-war cinemas which remain standing, the Belgrave is scheduled for demolition, the Plaza is a snooker hall and restaurant, the State is unused, and the Gaumont Palace is currently empty having previously been a nightclub and is undergoing a stalled conversion to a religious centre. In Devonport the Forum, the only cinema there to survive the war, is now a bingo hall.

The Royal Cinema has been threatened with closure on a number of occasions when proposals for its demolition and replacement have been announced. In late 2016, a tower block with student accommodation and a hotel was proposed, and a year later plans appeared for a 'co-living' scheme, which once the neoliberal gloss is peeled appears to be a way to exploit those failed by a broken housing market, with a very 21st century slum. The Royal is unique in Plymouth- the only pre-war cinema to still operate, and indeed it is unique nationally as the only WR Glen cinema (out of a total of 67) to have operated continuously as a cinema since it was built. Long may the last picture house continue to serve the people of Plymouth."

Karl Parsons (Plymouth)

Bibiography

*Atwell D. (1980) '**Cathedrals of the Movies**' –*
The Architectural Press, London

*Chapman G. (2000) '**Cinema in Devon**'*
Devon Books, Tiverton

*Eyles A. (1993) '**ABC The First Name in Entertainment**'*
BFI Publishing, London

*Gould J. (2010) '**Plymouth Vision of a Modern City**' English Heritage, Swindon*

*Gray R. (1996) '**Cinemas in Britain**'*
Lund Humphries Publishers, London

*Harwood E. (1994) '**The Listing of Cinemas in English Heritage Conservation Bulletin**'*
Vol 22 pp8-9

*Paton Watson J. & Abercrombie P. (1943) '**A Plan For Plymouth**'*
Underhill, Plymouth

Twyford H.P. (revised by Robinson C.) 2005
'It Came to Our Door'
Pen & Ink Publishing, Plymouth

Plymouth Architectural Trust

The Royal, Plymouth's Cinema

Talk by Karl Parsons

Wednesday 7th March 2018, 5.45pm

Lecture theatre, Plymouth Athenaeum, Derrys Cross

Please join us for a talk about the history of the Royal (now Reel) Cinema, presented by Karl Parsons who is leading a community effort to envisage a viable future for the building.

The Royal Cinema was designed by the ABC Cinema 'in-house' architect WR Glen, and opened in 1938. Large for a late 1930s provincial cinema, it sat 2,404 and was fitted with what may have been the best Compton Organ installed in any cinema. Within a few short years many of the buildings nearby had been destroyed in the blitz, and the Royal Cinema was one of the few pre-war buildings mentioned by name in 'A Plan for Plymouth', which saw it forming the nucleus of a new entertainment district.

In the 1950s the ABC chain introduced live performances to its cinemas to counteract falling audiences, and the cinema (by now known as the ABC) saw many live acts including two visits by the Beatles. In the 1970s the building was subdivided, with the cinema reopening with three screens located above the foyer and in the former circle, while the stalls and stage were converted into a bingo hall. This secured its future through the 1980s, a period which saw the loss of many cinemas. It has been a Cannon Cinema, and an MGM, and is now under the Reel brand.

Karl's talk will take us on a virtual tour of the building, exploring its history and cultural heritage, with accompanying photographs showing rarely-seen remnants of original decorative detail and backstage areas that are currently hidden from view. Join us to learn more about ambitious plans to bring the building into community ownership, and become part of a growing local campaign to save The Royal.

Places are limited and must be booked in advance, RSVP to book

PAT members and non-members free

RSVP to hilary.kolinsky@gmail.com

or call 01752 604 199 to book a place

The Royal
Plymouth's Cinema

'It's More Than Just a Job'

"The Office!

When I first started work there, in 1992, technology hadn't been invented.

Ticket stubs were threaded on 3" needles, to be taken to the office at the end of the night...'Eff & Safety's worst nightmare. They were just perfect for stabbing irate customers!

The staff could be as rude back to said irate customers, without the fear of a complaining e-mail to HO.

The only office equipment was an old manual typewriter. A fax machine was installed later, but all the paper-work was done manually.

No tills in the cash desk & kiosk. The money was kept in little pots under the counter & staff had to have a good sense of mental arithmetic!

No computers, no booking system. Once all the films had started, the front doors were shut until the next shows. Queues would either wind right round the building, or snake down to mingle with the Drake, Odeon queues, then we had 30 mins to get everyone in before the films started."

Knickers to the new Bridget Jones!

THEY'RE an essential component of any girl's wardrobe, although most of the time they go unseen.

But thanks to the huge success of the tales of Bridget Jones, big pants are big news – and if you've got a pair hidden away at home, dig them out this weekend as they could earn you free cinema tickets.

To mark the release of the new Bridget Jones film, The Edge of Reason, the ABC Cinema in Plymouth is urging fans of the Chardonnay-swigging singleton to don a pair of giant pants when they come to see the movie this weekend.

Anyone brave enough to show up wearing big pants over their clothes from Friday, November 12 until Sunday, November 14, will receive a free guest ticket for a future film as compensation for their embarrassment.

That's not all: the ABC is using the release of the film to make some money for charity, and this weekend the cinema is donating 50p from the sale of each ticket for the Bridget Jones sequel to the World Cancer Research Fund.

Cinemagoers can also take advantage of cheaper tickets, as the cinema has cut its admission price to just £3, and all weekend there will also be competitions and a chance to win prizes donated by local businesses, including health club membership at Cannons and a romantic meal at La Tasca.

Staff at the ABC Cinema got into the Bridget spirit by pulling on some

Visiting Celebrities:

Daniel Day Lewis & Daley Thompson –

NOT impressed. Swanned in, swept up the stairs, with NO intention of paying their way.

The Four Tops –

Dressed in trackies and baseball caps, but dripping in gold jewellery.

Russ Abbott –

Lovely and very self effacing.

Rik Mayall –
Who my colleague told off for pulling funny faces, when actually she thought he was quite good looking.

Marti Pellow (ex Wet Wet Wet) –
Much taller than I expected.

Dave Hill (ex Slade) –
Much smaller than I expected, I blame the platform boots of the '70s.

<u>'Non-Smoking' Policy.</u>
In 1992, Everyone smoked in the building, mostly the staff. Amazing there was never a fire.
The new regulations came in, not that it affected the manager of the time, who would send out a member of staff to get her a bottle of wine & when anyone wanted to go to the office, there would be a pause, the sound of an air freshener, then the door opened to a sickly smell & a cloudy haze!!
When Vue opened, it was so quiet and boring, staff would go round the side of the building for a spliff, on the pretense of 'checking the exits'.

Cherrie Harvey (Employee – ABC/REEL, Plymouth)

"I worked here for a year and a half back in 2008, best job I had. I still watch films here because it's a part of history and it's better than the Vue Cinema."

Paul Smith (Plymouth)

"My grandma was the manageress there when I was small. She worked there for years."

Hellen James (Plymouth)

"Worked there for 12 years. Good charity events. Still take my niece there now."

Duncan Jago (Plymouth)

ABC staff rewarded for dedication

HALF a century of keeping movie fans happy has been rewarded with long service certificates for three employees of a Plymouth cinema.

The three women have worked for ABC cinemas for a total of 50 years and to mark their dedication they were presented with awards, gift vouchers and flowers.

Customer service assistant Maureen Bond has clocked up a grand total of 25 years' service at the Derry's Cross cinema.

Mo Body, the cashier/clerk, received an award for 15 years' service and customer service sales assistant Cherrie Harvey has completed 10 years' service.

But the dedicated trio were not the only ones in line for awards.

The cinema itself was recently presented with a prestigious Investors in People Award for 2002.

THANKED: Left to right, Mo Body, Maureen Bond and Cheri Harvey

Picture Paul Slater [illegible]

"I worked at the ABC and met some lovely celebrities.
My favourites had to be ***Patrick Cargill****,* ***Melvin Hayes*** *and* ***Terry Scott*** *when they were in 'The Wind In The Willows' at the Theatre Royal in '84/'85.*
We had a complimentary ticket system going the three gentlemen had used their free tickets, so myself and another cashier said they could use our comps, they thanked us watched the film and went on their merry way.
A few hours later the trio appeared bearing gifts. They gave my colleague and myself a beautiful bouquet of flowers and a 5lb box of chocolates and thanked us for our kindness earlier.
Such lovely gentlemen, we met many famous faces at the ABC and have to say all but one were lovely down to earth people.
Happy memories of my time working there."

Sue Whiteman-McKinney (Plymouth)

" I worked at the cinema from December 1998 till June 2001 (approx.) whilst I was a student at Marjons. I met my future husband, Marc Howell there who was also working whilst studying at Plymouth University.

We are both originally from Plymouth and have childhood memories of going to the cinema as children. I remember especially queuing to see 'Jurassic Park' with my cousin Kelly, all the way to the old Ballard swimming pool and we still got a seat. I also remember everyone clapping at the end of the film - something I'd never seen before.

Both Marc and I have very fond memories of working at the cinema- the staff- who were a fantastic team of people, the loyal customers who stood by the cinema with the opening of Warners/Vue and all the threat of closure as a result and also the shock closing of the Odeon Drake cinema - most people thought it would be us first!).

It was honestly the best job I've ever had. Both my husband and myself went onto become teachers and moved to North East Derbyshire but we still visit family in Plymouth and are looking forward to taking our two children for their first visit to the ABC/Reel cinema in May when we are next visiting.
It really felt a very special place obviously, sentimentally as I met my future husband and father of our children there but also it was just a lovely place to work with a great bunch of people. The building was so interesting and beautiful. I remember American tourists being amazed by its history. We were all terrified of locking up screen 2 too because of the reported 'ghost'!
We will be so very sad if it's knocked down. Thank you for what you are doing. It is nice to know that others love that place like we do."

Maxine Gachagan (North East Derbyshire)

TICKE
NT BAR SERV

EXIT
CREAM
CALIPPO

"REEL GOOD FUN"
ghost spotting
alcohol
pauls grotto
bowling
REEL
CHRISTMAS
BASH
bouncy castle
lap dancing
karaoke
party food
cage fighting
west indian throat singing
14 . 12 . 08
musical chairs
DOLBY SR
only at the Reel cinema Plymouth
dts

THE PHANTOM MENACE: Manager Carole Nelson investigates the ABC's Screen Two, where spectral phenomena have been reported

It's just another ghost story – or is it?

GHOSTLY apparitions, unexplained noises and doors that unlock themselves – Plymouth's ABC Cinema is showing a lot more than just the latest big-screen epics these days.

The cinema has experienced a number of spooky goings-on, which staff say get noticeably worse when the cinema is showing a scary film.

Stories have been circulating for years that the cinema is haunted, with one suggesting it could be the ghost of an actress who committed suicide in one of the old dressing-rooms at the rear of the building, which used to be a theatre. Manager Carole Nelson said there had been reports of ghostly sightings of a woman in a long red skirt and jacket with black braiding round the neck and arms. The apparition has become such a regular feature at the cinema that staff have even given her a name – Emma.

Staff have also noticed random cold spots in the cinema and seats which do not spring back to the upright position when not in use, giving the impression that someone is sitting in them.

All the sightings occur around the cinema's Screen Two, and when spooky films are shown the complex often suffers problems with its sound system.

Ms Nelson said many of the cinema's staff felt uncomfortable working in Screen Two, one even giving up his job because he was so unsettled. Customers had reported cold spots and the feeling of an unnatural presence.

Ms Nelson said the number of incidents had risen during screenings of Ring 2, a follow-up to the 2002 chiller about a cursed videotape. Since the film opened, a padlocked door has managed to unlock itself and cinemagoers have reported seeing a woman seated at the front of the house watching a film – but when the lights go up at the end of the film, she is not there. Other spooky films such as The Blair Witch Project, The Exorcist, The Others and The Gift have also seen an upturn in ghostly goings-on.

Ms Nelson said: "I don't even believe in ghosts, but these things just don't have any clear explanations. We'll just have to ride out the storm and hope there are no further reports, but I would like to reassure customers. These reports are quite rare, but if you are prone to believing in supernatural forces I can confirm no-one has been hurt or threatened in any way."

"I worked at the ABC as an usher in my student years from 1997 – 2000. It was a dream student job that combined flexible hours, lovely colleagues, and of course films. During that time the front of house team included Cherie, Ann, Vilma, Alan and Wendy, and students Saba, Anthony, Neil, Mark, Maxine, Simon and me. I hope some of them will see this and remember those days – it was a great crew.

Our bosses were then Manager - Carole, and Deputy Manager - Maureen (Mo).

At the time, smoking was still permitted in workplaces and I recall the staff room and Manager's Office were often thick with cigarette smoke. Mo had a unique talent for balancing a whole fag's worth of ash on the end of a cigarette whilst she planned

the staff rotas for the forthcoming week.

*The job of an usher unfortunately rarely involved watching complete films. Instead you had to piece them together in fragments caught between duties. You would always miss the start whilst collecting tickets from late-comers, and always catch the penultimate 2 minutes whilst waiting to open the screen doors as the final credits rolled. In between times we'd be were sweeping popcorn off the stairs, manning the kiosk, or checking in on each of the screens. As a result, only the closing scenes of popular late '90s films are etched on my memory forever. This will serve me well if the words of Morgan Freeman's Presidential speech in '**Deep Impact**' ever comes up in a pub quiz, but is otherwise of little use in everyday life. The worst film in this respect was '**Titanic**', which ran for months at the ABC, rather than the usual 2 weeks. If I never hear Celine Dion's 'My Heart Will Go On' again it will be too soon.*

Even though there was competition from the Odeon just a few doors away, and later from the Vue, it was still common for blockbusters in the late 1990's to sell out in the main screen for the opening weekend or longer. Weekend sell-out screenings were the most likely to require some crowd control, but troublesome teenagers could usually be silenced with a glare of the torch and a sharp shush. In a rambling cinema like the ABC it was also possible for cheeky kids to hide on the back stairs or in the loos between screenings and then sneak into the next showing for free.

We kept this in check, but I'm sure a few wiley youngsters managed to slip through the net.

In all the time that I worked at the ABC I never had the opportunity to see the old back of house dressing rooms, which were reputedly haunted. Occasionally Carole would trot out these ghost stories for the press. Though the cynic in me thought these tall tales were invented to get column inches for the ABC during quiet weeks, there was still something eerie about the deserted back corridors at the end of a night and I would scamper back into the relative comfort of the cinema screen pretty sharpish after locking the fire escape doors at closing time!

I'd love to see the long-term future of the cinema secured for the people of Plymouth. It was revelation to me that the original stage is still preserved behind the subdivision into screens 1 and 2 that were inserted in the 1970's, and this gives the building great flexibility for future re-use. The cinema holds so many memories for local people, myself included and it deserves a fine future that honours its place in hearts of Plymothians."

Photo: my old name badge, kept in a drawer for 20 years!"

Hilary Kolinsky (was Hilary Phillips)
ABC staff 1997 – 2000 (part-time)

TICKE
NT BAR SERV

Save Our Cinema'

"I have lived in Plymouth all of my life and like so many others the Reel Cinema holds many fond memories. This is why we must stop Plymouth City Council giving the go ahead to the upcoming proposals.
It is set to be demolished and replaced with a hotel, commercial units and student accommodation. I don't see the necessity for any of these things as there is already a plentiful supply of them all.
What is important is to maintain and preserve a character filled building that houses an affordable cinema for the people of Plymouth.
It's a beautiful 1930's Art Deco Building faced in stunning white Portland stone. There is so much history surrounding it including a visit from The Beatles in 1963!
Plymouth was flattened during The Blitz and we lost so many historic buildings. This is why it's so important to treasure and enjoy the ones we have left."

Debbie Colwill (Plymouth)

Our say...

THE Herald
THE VOICE OF PLYMOUTH

Closure would be Reel pity

70 YEARS of Plymouth history could come to a sad end with the rumoured closure of the Reel Cinema at Derry's Cross.

The former ABC is the city centre's last old cinema and the home of happy memories for many Plymothians.

As well as years of showing movies, news reels and Saturday cartoons from its opening in 1938, the building doubled as a theatre in the 1960s and 1970s, hosting top bands from The Beatles to Deep Purple.

Most cities have now lost their old cinemas as people flock to out-of-town developments.

Despite the revived popularity of cinema-going, the multiplex offering and the convenience of the "home cinema" is too great for the traditionals to compete with.

And Plymouth city centre would be missing out on a valuable chunk of custom as cinema-goers are no longer drawn into town.

The extra trade generated for neighbouring bars and restaurants would be lost at considerable cost.

It is a poor sign for the city's night-time economy as the credit crunch is bound to affect people's leisure spending in every way.

But the city still has much to shout about and must remain positive about its great offering for entertainment – by day and night.

The Plymouth Summer Festival includes many events which are free, from the fantastic fireworks championship on The Hoe to the Flavour Fest food extravaganza in the city centre.

There are numerous day festivals and city centre events which embrace communities and local talent.

Plymouth city centre has the Pavilions attracting world-class music acts and the Theatre Royal bringing West End shows to the West Country.

The rumoured closure of the Reel cinema marks the sad end of an era. But Plymouth still has much to enjoy.

"Took all 4 of my grandsons to this cinema for their first cinema experience. They still say they prefer to go to the 'old fashioned little cinema' to see their films when I take them to the cinema. GREAT CINEMA!!! GREAT MEMORIES!!

Taff 'Rockin' Bear' Evans (Plymouth)

*"It was the cinema I went to see '**Terminator 2**' in on my first day here for University, unfortunately having been there recently it has had no investment for a long time. Such a shame."*

Jonathan Wells (Plymouth)

"This cinema is one of very few stunning buildings left in Plymouth!
They are all being replaced by ugly student lets.
This is the only cinema left in Plymouth that's affordable and you don't need a mortgage to go and visit. It can't be closed!"

Lauren Weatherall (Millbrook)

"Plymouth is a uniquely 'twentieth century city', but one which sadly seems to be all too keen to erase its own history. I watched with dismay as the Hoe Centre was demolished, and on hearing of plans to demolish the Reel I felt I had to at least try and do something to save what I saw as a lovely old building.
Starting a Facebook group with two friends caught the attention of the local press, and from that initial publicity the strength of feeling within the city for this faded, slightly battered yet proud building was heartening to see. Cinema itself was a twentieth century phenomenon, and the Reel/ABC a wonderful example from the golden age of cinema construction.
*I grew up in Pembrokeshire, and the cinemas of my childhood were quite small and decidedly down at heel. Nonetheless they were magical places, where you could escape from the real world and into the one created in a studio. Where I saw '**Watership Down**' (and as an eight year old shed a few tears) has since been demolished, as has where I watched '**Star Wars-Episode IV'**.*
Moving to Portsmouth I enjoyed the Cannon Cinema (also an ABC designed by W.R. Glen), far larger than the ones of my childhood and though altered it still retained a sense of 1930's glamour. From there I went to London with its many cinemas old and new, but the one I remember most fondly is the tatty Elephant and Castle Coronet, another old ABC which though operating successfully as a venue until January 2018 is due to be demolished as part of the redevelopment of the nearby shopping centre.
Arriving in Plymouth the ABC and the nearby Drake were a pleasure to find and visit, but since then the Drake has of course been demolished, and while there are many more screens in the city now, with more on the way, it is the ABC which is both affordable and friendly, retaining that magic, that glamour, that sense of occasion which its had since July 1938. Long may it continue serving the city."

Karl Parsons (Plymouth)

*"I had my first trip to the cinema for my 5th birthday here! '**Return of the Jedi**' was the film of choice.
As a teenager I went many times with friends and more recently I took my two young children too see '**Finding Dory**'."*

Sarah Harden (Plymouth)

*"It was in the ABC around 1978 that I discovered a well aimed salted peanut could cause havoc during an airing of Irwin Allen's '**The Swarm**'."*

Andy Melvin (Plymouth)

Now showing at a cinema near you

RICHARD BRANSON bought the MGM chain for £200 million.

He's my hero, says award-winning Plymouth MGM manager Carole Phillips, right

by JUSTIN WARR

Tycoon takeover will keep city jobs safe, says MGM manager

THE MGM cinema in Plymouth is in line for a face-lift following tycoon Richard Branson's multi-million-pound takeover of the company.

A Virgin spokesman confirmed that tens of millions will be spent improving the 116 MGM cinemas nationwide.

Richard Branson, owner of Virgin, beat off stiff competition from other firms to land the nationwide MGM chain for £200 million after it was offered for sale.

Virgin cinema signs will replace the MGM banners at Plymouth within 18 months.

Plymouth's ambitious MGM manager Carole Phil-lips is delighted at the takeover, which she says secures dozens of jobs at the picture-house.

She said: "Richard Branson has always been a hero of mine. He has a very dynamic approach and I am delighted. MGM did have a big investment plan and it looks like Virgin will take that on board.

"I believe jobs are secure here too."

Carole, 30, took on the role of Derry's Cross MGM manager last September and was the first woman to win the nationwide MGM Manager of the Year Award after bidding to attract more cinema-goers with Saturday-morning children's shows and late-night screenings.

Since the popular Plymouth Derry's Cross cinema opened in 1938, there have been four managers and its name has already changed three times – from The Royal to the ABC to the MGM.

Famous stars to have appeared live at the cinema when it was a theatre and music venue include Sir Cliff Richard in 1962 and the Rolling Stones in 1964.

The Stones, described as a "controversial" band and condemned by Plymouth parents as a bad influence on children, played at the ABC in the summer of 1964.

Chart-topping PJ Proby also visited the ABC in 1965.

Other artists who performed there included Cilla Black and Tom Jones.

REEL

*"When I was 17 they showed the film by Slade the group. The film was called '**Slade in Flame**' and was released in January 1975 in the year that I would reach 17."*

As I was working in the Record Department of an Electrical shop in the city centre - the record bar and listening booths x2

were in a shop called Albert E Ford - we were given tickets for a preview and to meet the group afterwards and myself and another assistant (Carol Tanner) went.
It will be a shame to lose it..."

Julie Cross (Plymouth)

"I went once, it was incredibly run down, had uncomfortable seats - but did sell beer!!"

Luke O'Neill (Plymouth)

"It is an important part of my life to be honest. I'm sure we've all been there with best friends, relatives that have passed on and not to mention first dates at the ABC/Reel.
When my sister and I were in the sixth form at school, some of my favourite memories as a teenager were 'mitching off' PE and going to the cinema with my sister. Think it was every other Wednesday ha ha x
*Okay I've just checked through some of my cinema tickets. I saw '**Lord of The Rings**' at Vue (oh dear). However I did watch two '**Matrix**' films at the ABC, '**Pirates of The Caribbean**' and '**Sleepy Hollow**'.*
*I watched '**Indiana Jones and The Last Crusade**' there. Sure I saw two '**Back to The Future**' films and most of the '**Star Trek**' films there. I also watched '**James Bond Quantum of Solace**' and '**The X Men**' movies there. I might be wrong about some of those, but I definitely saw '**Mars Attacks**' ha ha.*
I have kept most of my cinema tickets from 1990s up to now so I will check through them.
*Unfortunately the most recent film I saw was '**Trolls**'. However it was my nephew's first visit to a cinema so that is an important memory for me and hopefully he will remember it too.*
*I want to go see '**Trainspotting 2**' there this week.*

Kelly Forsyth (Plymouth)

*"I went there on reluctant date age 12 to see '**Top Gun**'.
My date was so short he didn't pull off the 15 rating and meekly went home as I joined my friends inside the cinema to weep over Goose...there was no second date
#nosurprise #baddate #feelabitmean"*

Jane Pierce (Plymouth)

"It's a shame to see iconic building with such history destroyed."

Anne-Marie Cole (Plymouth)

*"Remember queuing for 3 hours around the outside of the building to see '**Grease**'. The second time was only about an hour or so. By the fourth time I think I went straight in.
Saw my first 'X' movie there, '**Saturday Night Fever**' in 1977 when I was only 14. Went with my Mum because I thought they probably wouldn't check my age & they didn't. My friends were so jealous. Good times."*

Liz Walch (Plymouth)

"To be honest I only went in there a couple of times hence nothing to tell really, but I love the old building and look forward to read everything about it.
Basically it's a lovely old building and I'm fed up with our old buildings being demolished and thrown away like rubbish!
They are our history.
Too many are being destroyed, so much so that we won't have any left soon. Shame on the people who give permission to have them taken away from us instead of planning around them."

Jennifer Hobbs (Plymouth)

*"I remember going to watch '**Grease**', but the queues were all down the street and the Drake had queues a quarter of the way down Union Street, so watched '**Convoy**' in the Odeon (or was it still Top Rank at the time?)*
Great venue, it should be saved! Always warm with nice staff.
We go to the REEL quite frequently, hope it stays!"

Ian Randell (Exeter)

"Got kicked out when I was 12 for throwing popcorn..."

Joshua Dingle (Torpoint)

*"I have watched many great films there including '**The Dam Busters**', '**The King and I**', '**Ben Hur**', many of the early '**Carry On**' Films, '**Zulu**', and most recently '**the Lego Batman Movie**'.*
I will be devastated if this Cinema closes, as I have many happy memories of my time there and would like to make many more with my grandchildren."

Leslie Parsons (Plymouth)

"Unlike now, where the cinema has become an everyday event for couples on dates or nights out with mates, back when I was young in the '70s it was a REAL treat to go to the cinema.
My parents couldn't afford to take a family of four children to the cinema on a regular basis, so I will always remember, especially on a Sunday my parents would suggest we went for a walk around the town centre, window shopping as this was back in a time when no shops opened on a Sunday.
As we meandered our way from the top of the town to the bottom, us children would nudge and whisper with excitement because we knew what might happen next.
Sure enough as we approached the bottom end of Royal Parade my mother would announce that we were all going to the cinema!!
We'd all scream with excitement, the best feeling ever.
This is why films mean so much to me even now...

*As I grew older I could afford to go with my friends and saw '**Evil Dead 2**', five times in a weekend at the ABC cinema. '**Robocop**', three times in one day there too.*
*They had the UK premier of '**Indiana Jones and the Last Crusade**' with the Lord Mayor of Plymouth in attendance. John Rhys-Davis was supposed to attend but couldn't make it so sent a recorded message, I still have the program and ticket stub somewhere.*
*Plus there were the 'all-nighters'. I saw the '**Friday the 13th**' all-nighter twice and the '**Alien**' and '**Aliens**' films back to back.*
Great times great memories in a great and historic venue.
The ABC/Reel cinema is an important part of Plymouths heritage."

Jason Bloomfield (Plymouth)

"I love this place, the staff are always so nice to me and I love the vintage feel when I go in there."

Harley Quinzel (Plymouth)

"This picture house was called the Royal when I was a kid. Saturday morning pictures was great, proper upstairs if you were rich everything about it was great, even the Gaumont in Union Street and the Odeon in New George Street.
I know life goes on, but sometimes these places still have a place in our times, shame councils can't wait to pull them down...
This was part of the Royal - note that was there before it was bombed in the war."

Sylvia Jolley (Plymouth)

"Actually making the cinema a comfortable experience would probably aid in saving it. It's awfully kept, the staff are rude and it simply cannot compare with the Vue.
The only saving grace is the price. But unless they buck up their act, it's always going to be worth that few extra quid to go to the Vue.
Clean it up, renovate it and actually make it a pleasant comfortable cinema experience, then it might actually be worth saving."

Charlotte Adamson (Plymouth)

"My best friend scared the light of days out of me, but the film was amazing."

Elinor Wilson (Plymouth)

*"I saw all the '**Elvis**' films there. I used to watch all the performances as you didn't have to leave after the film finished; happy memories!"*

Jenny Jones (Plymouth)

*"1984 aged 9 - Every weekend from '**Ghostbusters**' to '**Back to the Future**', my cinematic childhood built on this place and the Drake."*

Michael Murray (Plymouth)

*"I went and saw '**Grease**' there as well. I still have the LP to this film. Good old days!"*

Pearl Westgate (Plymouth)

"I love this cinema, I go there every time a new kids movie comes out 'cos my son cant go to The Vue because it's too loud. So essentially when/if they take this place away my kids will never get to go to the cinema again!! Sad days."

John Cooper (Plymouth)

*"I remember going there with my best friend and a few others to a Saturday double bill. We watched '**Pretty in Pink**' and '**Top Gun**'. Saturdays were our 'grown up' days. I remember wearing a black jumpsuit and faux fur jacket and then when the films finished we all went to KFC to spend 99p on a chip and gravy dip meal.*
I am 43 now and still best friends with my friend I actually met at about 5 years old.
Why can't the fat cats leave our beautiful buildings alone, they are what makes Plymouth amazing."

Paula Moran (Plymouth)

"Why can't they just leave it alone?
There is a need for a cheaper, in town, alternative to the £15 hotdog, Leisure Park, soulless multiplex.
My kids love the twisting corridors to the toilets.
And that we can walk there if the mood takes us."

Luis Escobar (Plymouth)

"Great, I like!"

Aurelio Violante (Genève, Switzerland)

"I have seen many films there, the last being Saturday.
*We took our little boy to see '**the Batman Lego Movie**' with his Grandad and cousins.*
My Dad saw his first film there 61yrs ago, at the age of 9."

Elaine Parsons (Plymouth)

*"When I was about 10, or 11, my friend and I wanted to see '**True Love**' with Grace Kelly but it was a 12 certificate. So we asked total strangers to take us in for the afternoon matinee. We met up inside.*
Looking back our mothers didn't seem bothered that we had done that, it would be a different story today."

Susan Cotter (Plymouth)

*"I went to see '**Grease**' there. I spent an anxious time in the queue, as I wasn't officially old enough to get in and didn't look old enough either.*
*My friend Julie Fray and I took her younger brother and sister to see the first '**Star Wars**' film.*
*I was scared out of my wits seeing '**Friday 13th**' there.*
So many cinematic memories!"

Amanda Jones (Plymouth)

"I've been to the ABC more times than I'd like to remember! Back in the early '70s my friends and I got in underage to see many 'X' rated films- naughty!

Sally Ann West (Plymouth)

*"I remember queuing to see '**Grease**' in the late seventies.
Going to the ABC club on Saturday's and seeing Sacha Distel with my friend Leigh McCarthy, along with lots more happy visits.
My sister was one of the lucky ones who saw the Beatles, I was too young at the time!!!"*

Janet Hawkins (Plymouth)

*"Lovely memories of meeting my husband there on our first date.
Took my children there to see many films."*

Verna Emery (Plymouth)

"Saw my first movie as a teenager (no supervision) here, 'Young Einstein'."

Wes Ashton (Plymouth)

"I used to go there sixty years ago, good memories."

Lilly May-Stephens (Tavistock)

"I've been there so many times and it's always been an amazing bit of architecture."

Bailey Whiteway (Plymouth)

*"This building brings art, culture and entertainment to those who maybe can't afford a night out at a multiplex, in a beautiful, authentic setting.
A huge part of my childhood, and should not be replaced by another bright, shiny (but sterile) new build."*

Ben Smart (Minehead)

*"I went to see '**the Exorcist**' with Caroline. I was scared witless. Everyone who knows me, knows I hate scary films."*

Christine Springett (Fareham)

*"Beautiful building inside and out. With a little money and time it could be back to its former glory.
Also the only affordable thing to do with the children on a weekend."*

Cheryl Portman (Plymouth)

*"I believe we should hold on to as many period buildings as possible in Plymouth. We have so little pre-war architecture it would be a shame to lose this Art Deco landmark.
By all means repurpose it, but save the building!"*

Caroline Coon (Plymouth)

"I'm signing because Plymouth has only so few 'pre second world war' buildings left in city centre area, that it would be catastrophic destroying on purpose this significant icon."

Stefan Krause former Plymouth City Centre BID Manager (Sturminster Marshall)

*"I don't go to the cinema often but when I do, I use the Reel.
They don't rip you off with ticket prices or food and drinks.*

Alexander Taylor (Torpoint)

'CURSE': *Cinema staff drop like flies after medical comedy hits screens*

Laughter's the worst medicine

■ by WILLIAM TELFORD

IT'S no laughing matter – since a Plymouth cinema started showing the medical comedy Patch Adams it's been hit by a spate of staff injuries.

Carole Nelson, manager of the ABC Cinema, Derry's Cross, has lost three members of her 22-strong, part-time team to aches and strains, and has even been injured herself.

She is suffering from a trapped nerve in her shoulder, but has been continuing to work at the cinema, which is showing the new Robin Williams vehicle Patch Adams.

The mirthful movie tells the true story of a madcap medical student who believes laughter is the best medicine.

Carole said staff at the cinema are trying to grin and bear the pain of their injuries.

The sick list includes customer services staff member Antony Hopkins, who has been off work for a week with tonsillitis and a football ankle injury. Colleague Marc Howell, with a dislocated shoulder that needed an operation, is also off work.

And another customer service staff member, Neil Bellamy, was sidelined with an ankle injury, caused playing rugby.

Carole said cinema employees had seen the side-splitting comedy, certificate 12, and were taking Dr Adams' movie advice.

Joke

She added: "You have got to laugh it off and joke about it. It seems to be working.

"The Patch Adams story is a real heart-warmer. The movie has a real feel-good sense to it, but I'm becoming concerned about the number of staff coming down with one injury or another. I think I may have to ask the St John Ambulance to visit us more often and only hope I don't have to call out 'is there a doctor in the house?'."

Carole is now hoping the

"I make regular use of this excellent little cinema. The soulless Vue alternative doesn't even come close."

Luke Borley (Plymouth)

"Restore it to its glory in the same way as the Prince Charles cinema in London."

Gary Chester (Prestwich)

"Because we have a habit of destroying lovely buildings, to then regret at a later date."

Roger Day (Plymouth)

"Also when I booked up to see ***'The Mask'*** *film, in 1994, the staff dressed up as the character and played around with us! Great times!"*

Tristan Michael Tozer (Plympton)

"Reel Cinema is my 'go to' place and represents a group of happy and cherished memories.
It reminds me that the building has been loved by the people of Plymouth for such a long time.
How does a city retain its identity if you remove its history."

Carlton Rhodes-Neale (Plymouth)

"We need a diverse, lively, city centre that creates a built legacy to be proud of, and acknowledges the beautiful buildings that already exist. An 'over dominance' of student flats will ruin this."

Val Woodward (Plymouth)

*"One of my fondest memories was going to see '****Lemon Popsicle****', little 'risque' back then. Probably be an age 12 or something now. Anyway, it was an 'X' cert and my friend and I were about 15 I think, so we dressed up, made up, and got in!*
Learned a few things that night and couldn't wait to go to school and brag about our night."

Christine Ewings (Plymouth)

*"I remember going to see '****E.T.****' but the queue for the film was around the block. So we ended up going to see '****TRON****' instead.*
*History has proven '****TRON****' was far better than '****E.T.****'*
I also got away with saying my first swear in front of my mum, (twat, if anyone's interested)."

Daniel Southwould (Plymouth)

*"Remember my first cinema trip aged eight here to watch '**Flash Gordon**'!! The queue was right round the building to get in!!"*

Tracy Davis (Plymouth)

"Too many buildings are being lost in Plymouth's 'student centric ' development - time to save iconic buildings."

Alan Pottinger (Plymouth)

"This building survived WW2 and for many it is a link with that time and after. It's replacement, if and I sincerely hope it doesn't, architecturally beggars belief and should be refused on the grounds of ugliness. This cinema provides good family entertainment at an affordable price. Instead of demolition it should be restored to its former glory."

Andy Graves (Plymouth)

*"We were in there this afternoon. Lovely warm friendly place and affordable prices.
Please keep this cinema open."*

Joyce Westlake (Plymouth)

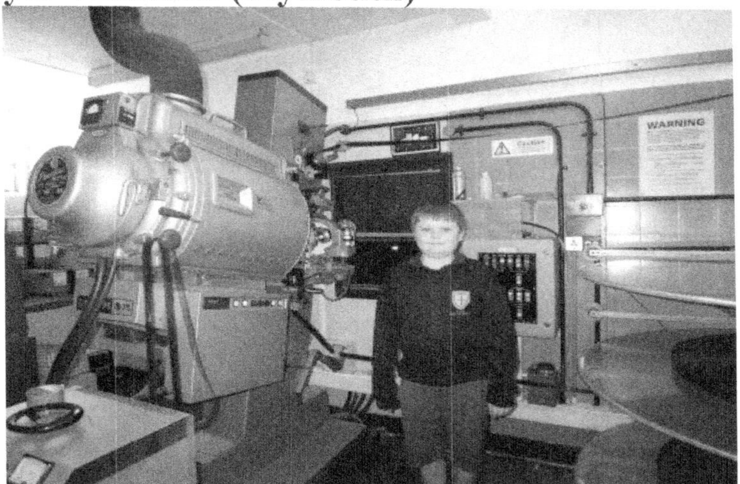

Cian (son of Photographer Beverley Kinsella at 10yrs old in 2008)

"This building is an important part of the city's fabric. Now it's use as a cinema is enjoyed by all. To be able to easily catch the bus into town and go to see a film is a bonus. Save this treasured building."

Linda Davidson (Saltash, Cornwall)

"Aside from the fact that it's cheaper than the awful Vue cinema complex, this cinema is an institution, a much valued part of our historic city's architectural landscape. Please, please don't tear it down!"

Laurence Birch (Plymouth)

"Plymouth has lost so many of its beautiful buildings.
It's time to save what we have left.
It's shocking how Plymouth is losing its identity and being filled with boring square concrete buildings and we've surely got enough student accommodation by now. Plymouth is an old city and should be treated with dignity it deserves."

Sharon Simpson (Plymouth)

"The monstrosity known as the 'Civic Centre' is protected, yet places like this are not.
PCC selling out and destroying Plymouth's history piece by piece. You're doing a better job than the Nazis did."

Sean Clark (Plymouth)

"It is the most amazing place, like walking back in time and being immersed in history - even when you go to see a modern movie."

Ruth Mielek (Ivybridge, Devon)

"Too many historic buildings in the city are being demolished to make way for students, while the Civic Centre stands empty, but LISTED."

David Lillicrap (Plymouth)

"The City needs a central cinema."

Barry Kirkman (Calstock)

*"It's a beautiful old building with a live in ghost apparently. Plus I have good memories of many a snog in the back row!
We need to keep some memories please...."*

Heather Shazell-Tomas (Plymouth)

"We need this more than we need more student accommodation! This building is of architectural significance and should be saved."

Sandra Williams (Plymouth)

*"I like having a reasonably priced cinema which has character. More people will support it if you just spend some money doing it up instead of tearing down!
Check out the Electric or Everyman Cinema in other towns for amazing inspiration!!
Lorenzos is a lovely building too."*

Sophie T. (Plymouth)

*"It holds a lot of childhood memories, which I now want to pass onto my children...
It's an absolutely stunning building inside (all be it needs a bit of TLC) which you hardly ever see in Plymouth anymore.
It has reasonable prices that cater for the people of Plymouth - unlike the Vue, which is very expensive.
We have enough 'student accommodation' being built in Plymouth left right and centre. How about the people of Plymouth come first for once????"*

Samantha Scott (Plymouth)

"This cinema means so much to so many of us, we don't use the big modern cinemas as we like our small local cinema."

Suzanne Edgar (Plymouth)

"I love the Reel Cinema! I love that it feels like stepping back in time and I hate the Vue because it is 'placeless'!"

Fiona Nicholls (Plymouth)

"Too many buildings are being lost in Plymouth's 'student centric ' development - time to save iconic buildings."

Alan Pottinger (Plymouth)

"Everyone goes to a cinema and this is part of Plymouth's history."

James Freeman (Oxfordshire)

"I went to this cinema a few years ago and I just loved the style, the ambience and the friendly welcoming staff.
Unfortunately the Compton organ had been removed but because it is one of the last large cinemas from the thirties that is left - and Art Deco at that - its protection should be guaranteed.
Having worked in multiplex cinemas, I have seen in the last 30 years how these thirties icons have been removed from the high street landscape. Those that are left now in the country should be protected -I support this petition to keep this cinema.
I used to be a Senior Film Booker working in the head offices of two multiplex companies - hopefully KC Sauri who runs this cinema and who I know personally, will keep this cinema running as long as he can. But I obviously don't know the circumstances of the minute details of the lease or freehold."

Mike Baxter (Trowbridge)

"This is a beautiful cinema that deserves to be cherished. It offers affordable prices and a different atmosphere to most commercial cinemas."

Katie Beauchamp (Plymouth)

"Do not pull the REEL down.
I use this cinema to see all the film I want to see. It is far better than the VUE or any of the new ones and a piece of history and the 'architecture' of the place."

Marion Pearse (Plymouth)

"This building has been around for years.
I know that loads of people like to visit and use this REEL cinema just because of its original state. I personally love the place. It needs to stay!!"

Kelly Lillicrap (Plymouth)

"I have fond memories of queuing round the block as both a child and a mother to see the latest films.
It's a fabulous building. We are losing to many of our heritage buildings."

Lisa Morrow-Mayer (Plymouth)

"This is a super building and a super cinema, offering a family alternative and a slice of Plymouth's architectural heritage."

Bill Wroath (Plymouth)

"It is full of memories, I don't want it to become on."

Abigail Marker (Plymouth)

"It may not seem like much, but when the only other cinema in Plymouth is more expensive, you do start to care. Plus it's not a bad place to catch the latest films."

Laura Reinbach (Plymouth)

"I agree that profit, employment and attractions to the city is incredibly important, but with so many empty sites and underdeveloped properties in the centre of Plymouth I cannot grasp their desire to destroy such a historic building which has contributed to so many memories.
It could be such a wonderful building again with a little love and attention.
Plymouth should be holding on with both hands to the historic buildings, especially this one with such beautiful Art Deco features."

Lorraine Carroll (Plymouth)

"There is enough student accommodation."

Ann West (Plymouth)

"Save this beautiful old Art Deco building, it's a great way of having a cheap evening out."

Angela Buckland (Plymouth)

"I agree we need to try and save old buildings in Plymouth since we have so few left after the combined efforts of the Luftwaffe and old City Corporation (forerunner of City Council).
The modern identikit buildings replacing them seem to be flimsily built and lacking in beauty and grace in their design e.g. Jury's Inn, Exeter Street and most of the modern flats on Sutton Harbour, modern flats at top of North Hill by Hill Park Crescent etc."

Will Tall (Plymouth)

"This building is part of our history and should be protected as such."

Ryan Lawton (Plymouth)

"Not everyone can afford the prices of the only other cinema we have in Plymouth with tickets about £12.50!
It gives the chance for families on lesser incomes to be able to enjoy family 'time out' without breaking the bank.
This is a lovely old building which needs a bit of TLC.
Again Plymouth City Council do not realise there is not a lot of its history left and what there is, they want to knock down."

Patricia Moody (Plymouth)

"Good for large families, Vue is too expensive."

Jamie Brogan (Torpoint, Cornwall)

"Lovely cinema I'd rather use this than the other big one."

Sam Diamond (Plymouth)

"I believe that history should be preserved."
Fred Chamness (Kissimmee, Florida)

"I just enjoy the films and I love the style of the building. I'm helping by sharing it to my friends etc."
Kathy Endacott (Plymouth)

"Fond memories of this cinema when I lived in Plymouth."
Theo Christian (Gateshead)

"It is full of memories, I don't want it to become one."
Abigail Marker (Plymouth)

"We do not need more student accommodation!!!
And it's cheaper than Vue!!!"
Danny Daniels (Plymouth)

"Some buildings deserve to be saved."
Vikki Clarke (Saltash)

"I have been going to the Reel Cinema for many years and love the character of the place - far more attractive and interesting than the modern cinema complexes!
Given that Plymouth lost so many of its old buildings during the war, it seems a great shame to lose this one as well.
Restoring it to it's former glory would make it a 'Reel' attraction within the city and preserve the heritage of the area.
Plymouth does not need more student accommodation or hotels so there is really no justification to lose the cinema!"
Karen Treasure (St Columb)

"A city's 'progress' isn't determined by the number of students it can house & the number of hotels a city has.
It isn't more important than the city's history & heritage."
Jim Dwyer (Plymouth)

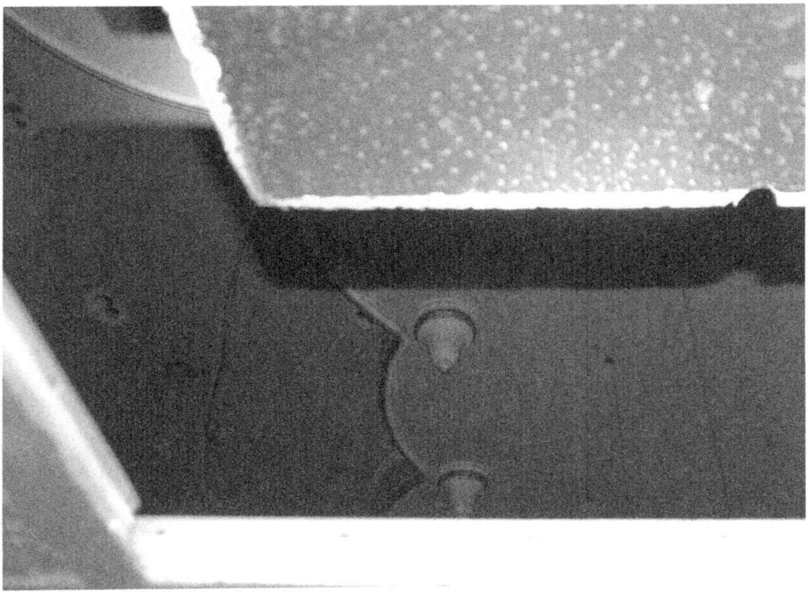

"I remember my birthday parties here and meeting with friends to watch the latest movies."
Kayleigh Osborne (Plymouth)

"Used to love going here as a kid & now plump for THIS cinema to take MY kids to.
*Most recent visit was '**The Force Awakens**' & '**Rogue One**'."*
Sher Smith (Plymouth)

*"I remember going to see '**Batman Vs Superman**' and people at the back trying to set the chairs on fire.*
Magical."
Steve Sargeant (Plymouth)

"I'm not sure what to say other than it being a good, affordable cinema in a fantastic building.
I will however say that this is likely merely another step in the council's plans to sell out the entire damn town, and that frankly, they should either listen to the people instead of their pockets or go jump off the Hoe and keep swimming until they can't hear either of them anymore."

Jonjo Wallis (Plymouth)

"Clive the manager always seemed nice and the staff (mainly older ladies) seemed very friendly.
*As an adult, I took my now wife to see '**Titanic**' on our 1st date. Sitting in the back row of Screen 2 with my mate Steve and his partner Sam, watching the dramatic scenes of Jack slipping away, people crying and my mate Steve moaning at the people getting upset.*
These memories will obviously make the Cinema special to me. Add that the Beatles played here (biggest band in the world) and Morecambe & Wise (comedy heroes) just adds that little bit extra to this amazing building and Cinema history."

Andy Gillies (Plymouth)

"Had my first date with my first love there.
Remember kissing round the corner, waiting for the room to be cleaned and opened, then having to go watch the film again so we could actually watch it.
Gonna miss the place very much, more memories there than bloody Vue - rip off."

Christopher Sutton (Plymouth)

"Many girl dates after school with best friends.
I love this cinema, it's ridden in old memories, inside is still so beautiful.
Such a shame for it to be going, Plymouth is being ruined by student flats ☺"

Amanda 'Moo' Rodgers (Plymouth)

Paul Gregory with a celebration cake and staff from the MGM cinema

Showing films for 30 years

*"This is THE BEST cinema in Plymouth, hand's down.
So much character, best value, great film selection. Who needs cup-holders anyway?!
To see it demolished would be unbelievably sad. I understand that development has to happen to stop everyone calling Plymouth a 'shit-hole' that never managed to get back on it's feet after the Blitz - but there has to be a better way to do it than to tear down city treasures like this.
Build around it for fuck's sake!....... Please!"*

Matt Koch (Plymouth)

"This is the only cinema we can afford to go to and it really is charming. The Vue is far too expensive and loud!"

Mandy Powell (Plymouth)

"This one time that has been in my head for years was not long after I started secondary school.
*I went there with my then boyfriend and we went to see '**Ace Ventura - When Nature Calls**' but they could not show it as there was a technical problem with it so we all got out of our seats and went downstairs.*
Everyone was kicking off saying that they wanted their money back. One guy started having a 'rite go' and me and my boyfriend just said –
'Lets get r money and go'
At the time it wasn't so funny but looking back on it now it is. Am not with that boy now, I think that we broke up not long after but that's how it goes when you are that young.
Now I am happily married with 3 kids, so not much time 4 things like that anymore. Lol.
Oh the good old days hey? Lol."

Claire McLatchie (Plymouth)

"I've been going to this cinema for over 30 years. It has always been and always will be my favourite cinema."

Mark Clevett (Plymouth)

"Spoke to my Dad to-day (96 years old).
His memory tells of his aunt and uncle running the Wellington pub in Deptford place.
They had a son – Peter - who fell in the fire and died. After the wake in the pub, close family all got on a charabanc and went to the picture house to see a film.
Dad's first experience of going upstairs in a lift.
With a bit of memory jogging, Dads stories keep coming. Dudley Savage, playing the Compton Organ and the radio programme 'As Prescribed' being broadcast from the picture house."

Felicity Barrett & Leonard Andrew (Plymouth)

"Some of my first memories are of this cinema. I lived in Plymouth as a child."

Lindsey Jackson-Kay (Plymouth)

"Plymouth can ill afford to lose such an iconic art deco cinema which is part of our history. An authentic pre-war cinema right in the city centre which should be celebrated and promoted not demolished for more student flats. Take a look at community cinemas in Kingsbridge and Christchurch for example to see what can be do."

Mark Brennan (Plymouth)

"We still use the cinema it's a shame if it was to go.
I have a disabled child who we take here.
She enjoys here - because she doesn't need to go out of the cinema to go to the bathroom.
It's never pushy to get in or out either so she feels safe."

Kate Hawcroft (Plymouth)

"The architecture of this era is iconic and timeless. Buildings like this, with such a rich history should be cherished, not disposed of.
Once they're gone, they will never exist again."

Phil Butler (Malvern)

"Gosh!! I used to go here as a child, the first cinema I ever went to.
Now I am behind the screen instead of watching it.
It will be sad if it goes, maybe the council should take on the responsibility of student accommodation.
There seems to be so many student digs that I wonder if it's all going to students? Or if the council should look at alternative accommodation for the locals?"

Sharron Foster (Newquay)

"It is an important part of the city's cultural heritage!"

Stephen Luscombe (Plymouth)

"I am signing because for me and my partner the REEL is the best cinema in Plymouth.
It is much cheaper than VUE and a lot calmer.
I'd hate to see it go."

Chelsea Sargeant (Plymouth)

"My first date in Plymouth was in that cinema, thanx for the memories."

Mohamed Hamid (Plymouth)

"It's a unique building and a good connection to the past. Put more money into the Mayflower 2020 celebrations.
It is a worthy cause.
The cinema is a lovely building, in a cultured area of Plymouth.
A helping hand given by a body with funding can really make the cinema shine."

William Shaw (Plymouth)

"Had my first date here when I was only 13, many girl dates after school with best friends.
I love this cinema, it's ridden in old memories, inside is still so beautiful. Such a shame for it to be going, Plymouth is being ruined by student flats."

Amanda 'Moo' Rogers
(Saltash, Cornwall)

"The REEL rocks."

Becky Curts (Plymouth)

"It is an important part of the city's cultural heritage!"

Stephen Luscombe (Plymouth)

"Whilst I understand that perhaps the cinema business itself may no longer be viable because of other competition, it would be a great shame to lose this historic building as a result.
Why can't the function of the building itself change, rather than it being knocked down? Much like the way the Royal William Yard has been used in a way that it was never designed for, and it is subsequently flourishing as a result.
Please sign this petition."

Matthew Fox (Plymouth)

"I want to keep the Reel cinema."

Deborah Ramson (Plymouth)

"Because it's a lovely place."

Jason Crandley (Plymouth)

"We all loved it, especially seeing our first 'AA' certificate (14+) at age 12, then one year later, our first 'X' (18+)"

Leonie Bates (Sutton, Surrey)

"When me and Matt went to see a film it was so scary, I fell asleep."
Connie Andrews (Plymouth)

"Concrete monstrosities get listed and yet anything with a little bit of design or history is flattened for more student flats...."
Arthur Hunter (Plymouth)

"Don't knock it down, so many great memories..."
Steve Westcott (Plymouth)

"I love coming to this cinema – it's the last one in Plymouth that resembles the 'old traditional' cinema.
My gramps used to work in one just like this and he always talks about how all the cinemas he remembers are disappearing and being replaced by the newer, larger cinemas.
I've always been able to say "well we still have the REEL in Plymouth"...
We always came to ABC/Reel, used to refill our refillable drink

from Subway and take our free cookie there while we watched the film!"

Abbie O'Brien (Saltash, Cornwall)

*"Me and my friends crying our eyes out while watching '**The Fault In Our Stars**'.*
I waited so long to see that movie, but it was worth it."

Sophie Wright (Plymouth)

"I first visited REEL cinema in May 2016
when my friend took me, after recently moving to Plymouth.
The whole building was phenomenal to look at inside and out.
So much history on our door-step and not to mention the prices are fair unlike Vue which is a rip off.
Such a lovely building and it was a big part of some peoples lives and it would be a huge shame to see it go.
I'd love to carry on visiting for years to come and make more amazing memories there."

Imogen Brook (Plymouth)

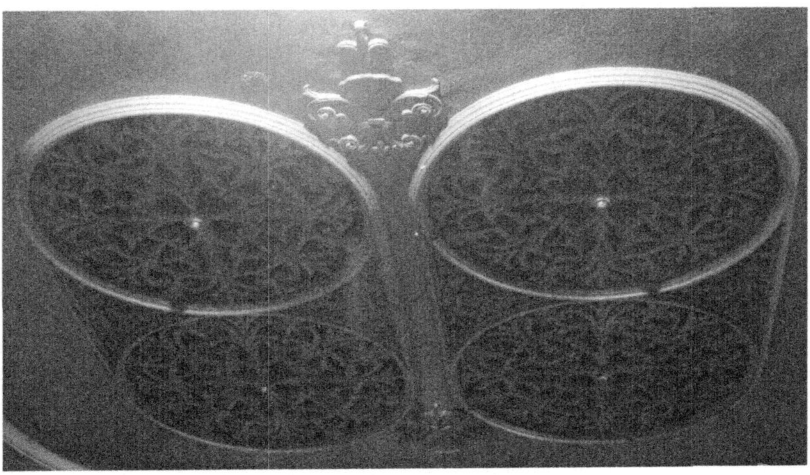

"Having just lost our two cinemas in Bournemouth, ABC and Odeon, this year and gained a modern square box full of restaurants
We are buildings, not lots of student flats.
I'm a not against modern buildings we need a good mix
If anyone wants to know more about cinemas go to Cinema Theatre Association website."

Philip Stevens (Christchurch)

*"Bunked in through the side door to see the '**Way of the Dragon**' in 1972 with my brother and his mate."*

Jan Wilson (Plymouth)

*"Took my nephew to a couple of kids club movies. ('**Planes 2**' and '**Home**') talked about them for weeks.*
Walked past the Vue to go to the slots (Ten Pin), he's never been to the Vue and he said, "I prefer the other one Uncle Paul."

Paul May (Plymouth)

"Being my local cinema growing up, I went to this cinema for at least 2 first dates and a last meet up of friends before some of us left to go to six-form.
*I saw the '**The Empire Strikes Back**' and '**View to a Kill**' with my dad, and the first film I was allowed to go to with my friends '**Who Framed Roger Rabbit?**'*
It was a symbol of teenage freedom.... Being able to walk from my house in Mutley - on my own - to meet my friends to watch a movie were my first steps towards independence."

Abi Gough (Plymouth)

*"I watched '**Beethoven's 2nd**" there for my 10th birthday in 1993 with 6 friends. Halfway through one friend went to the loo - only realised at the end that she hadn't come back.*
She had managed to get stuck in the toilet."

Karen Osborne (Plymouth)

*"The first film I saw in the 1960's was when it was called the ABC cinema. My first film in the ABC was '**Carry On Cruising**' in 1962."*

Brian Gimblet (Plymouth)

*"The cinema needs to be saved as it is a wonderful old building and has many memories to so many people in Plymouth.
Do we really need more student accommodation food outlets etc? Of course we don't and its about time Plymouth City Council stopped allowing this sort of thing to happen and stuck to their word on not allowing anymore student housing to be built; they have enough in my book."*

Mike Welcham (Plymouth)

*"This cinema is part of my childhood memories; I was a minor of the ABC.
Somehow it survived the bombing and was a centre of cinematic excellence and a major deliverer of entertainment which was much needed in the forties and beyond.
The queues used to wind right around the building.
I see now with adult vision that it is also a beautiful building, representative of the era when it was built."*

Patricia Kathleen Mary Read (UK)

*"Ah bloody don't tell me - They want it for student flats?
With the new plans for that new cinema complex at Bretonside, they will. But that place has so much history then again so did the Odeon, but PCC still got rid; anything PCC don't want to over take??"*

Michelle Clark Vincent (Plymouth)

"Needs to stay, better than the new heartless cinemas."

Mike Joslin (Plymouth)

"I've got happy times of this place."

Charmaine Oakes (Plymouth)

*"I remember queuing round the block to see '**Grease**' when it first came out. Didn't get in so went back the next day and queued for about 3 hours.*
Got in that time."

Cathy Sandle (Plymouth)

"Many have seen my posts about the ABC Royal cinema and its famous organ – I'm afraid it was me who removed the organ in 2006, which I would understand might not go down well with folk trying to save/preserve the building! However I was commissioned to remove it by Trinity College of Music who had bought it from the owners of the building. Unfortunately the project to install the organ into Blackheath Halls eventually fell through, due to a change of management plus the recession and the organ found itself seeking a new owner.
So, now to give some background about myself - My interest in this wonderful late thirties super-cinema and its organ goes back to as far as I can remember, despite the fact that I didn't come from Plymouth and didn't go there until our initial recce in 2005.
I was brought up in Essex in the 1960s and my Dad was a keen enthusiast of cinema organs and cinema buildings of the 1930s. He grew up when they were in their heyday and used to frequent some of London's finest. He was a keen amateur organist too and it was he who I inherited my interest in these amazing instruments from. Dad also used to collect photos of cinema organs, most of which from the great John Sharp collection, and one set he had was of the ABC Plymouth Compton organ, taken when Dudley Savage was still broadcasting his famous weekly programme from there. I distinctly remember looking at the photos of the organ console, the photos which I now have in my own collection. Dad always used to say how good that organ was - but I never imagined in my wildest dreams that I would end up owning it!
So, fast forward to 2005, by which time I had diversified from my career in television and video production to starting a business in pipe organ restoration - I had rekindled the interest

just after the millenium and had learned how these wonderful instruments work and how to restore and maintain them. Through a contact I was put in touch with the management at Trinity College of Music, which led to my team removing the rather forlorn organ in Feb 2006. However after the project was cancelled and Trinity wanted to dispose of it, I knew that the chances of finding a buyer who would keep it all intact were not very high, especially in the short time frame Trinity wanted, so I put my hand up and said I'd have it. I couldn't bare the thought of it being broken up for parts and I vowed to keep it intact and to find a new home for it if I possibly could. I have kept it in safe storage at my own expense for many years now, but at last am talking to a suitable venue who are interested and plans are being made.
Hopefully then this superb instrument will play again in the not too distant future - I will of course make sure that a plaque is positioned by the organ which tells of its origins in Plymouth, the famous radio programmes it featured on for thirty years and the magnificence of its former home.

Peter Hammond (London)

"Brilliant place, so much history, would be a shame to lose it. The cinema is much more than entertainment, it's one of the few things left in Plymouth that actually takes you back. Everything else has been altered, changed or destroyed. If Plymouth prides itself on history, why is it so quick to ruin what's left? Xx"

Kimm Hendy (Plymouth)

"I met lion cubs here xxx"

Becky Hendy (Plymouth)

"The Reel Cinema used to be known as the ABC Cinema. It was and is a marvellous grand classic 30's highly decorated cinema and Plymouth is very lucky that it still exists although somewhat modified now.
When I was a child, I used to be taken there with my brothers by our mother to see various films over the years, ice creams at the

intervals etc. and the magnificent huge red curtains.
There was always Pathe or Movietone News, a short first film, interval and then the main feature film.
A very special event for us, always enjoyed.
In the latter part of the 60's, a good night out with your girlfriend, was to go to the ABC and try and get in the back row right at the top of upper circle. Once the lights went down, very often the film was of secondary importance as we teenagers hogging the back rows had other things on our minds. It was all such fun. A good night out and at very little cost.
Also, of interest to me, was the fact that my best friend's dad was Dudley Savage, he was the resident organist at the ABC playing the fantastic Wurlitzer, like that in the Blackpool Ballroom today. He had a regular slot on BBC radio with a programme for the sick at home and in hospital called 'As Prescribed'. He presented and played requests for years including one for me when I happened to be very ill.
Great memories of a very special and now almost unique building that on no account should be demolished. Ideally it should be restored to its former glory as a single grand cinema and a theatre for shows such as when the Beatles visited Plymouth."

Adrian Mitchell (Plymouth)

"My Gran used to work here.
Best memories ever of visiting her in work as a child me and my sister's Becky Hendy, Georgie Young and Kimm Hendy."

Dahni Hendy
(Waterlooville, Hampshire, UK)

"2,404 souls on seats.
The Glory days.
Velvet curtains.
Emotion en-masse.
Eyes closed. Tears. Laughter.
Thrill shared with many in complex private ways under the anonymity of a darkness lit only by the 24 frames per second interrupting the canon of light cast down from behind.
Times past.
Changes must, made.
Survival, some might say.
But voluminous volume and commune contend with private choice in private spaces suiting private (on) demand.
And fuck the thought of being part of society.

A place was made.
Adapted.
Bettered and worsened.
A space exists still, though. A space which is a place for many.
Has been.
Is.
Could be.
Will be.
Ghosts and all. (Screen 2)."

Tim Mitchell (Plymouth)

SIXTIES STYLE: Dan Eagles and Antony Hopkins with their Minis

Picture Al Stewart 0513723

Mini-renaissance for cult film

NEVER mind the Self Preservation Society – the West of England Mini Owners Club is helping publicise the cult British film The Italian Job.

It has been 30 years since Michael Caine, his band of criminals and a fleet of Minis brought chaos to the streets of Turin in Italy.

But three decades on and the classic British caper movie is still wowing audiences.

To celebrate its 30th birthday, the ABC cinema at Derry's Cross is staging a week-long screening of the film – the only cinema in the South West to show the re-release.

And helping celebrations get into full swing were members of the West of England Mini Owners Club, who brought three Minis to the cinema.

Cult

Dan Eagles, spokesman for the ABC, said: "The whole Michael Caine thing has become a bit of a cult situation.

"The student population has really taken to it.

"I love the film and received the film on video as a present for Christmas, but you cannot beat seeing it on the big screen."

The Italian Job, which also stars Noel Coward and Benny Hill, and tells the story of a heist in the Italian city, is being shown at the cinema until Friday.

The movie has become a cult classic and the famous chase scene, which made the Mini ultra-fashionable, has recently been recreated in a TV commercial and a pop video by Welsh band the Stereophonics.

Butterkist

'Celebrity Endorsements'

"I was really shocked to hear that the cinema could be demolished as there seems to be little thought given to its heritage and indeed its uniqueness.
I know the cinema well as I spent a week in the building helping to remove the classic 'Compton' organ, which was taken for restoration and relocation.
I truly love buildings such as this and indeed this cinema has a place in
Plymouth's history and in my opinion should be preserved and more made of its wonderful history.
When places like this are destroyed they can never be replaced.
I think Dudley Savage (who I had the pleasure of meeting) will be turning in his grave at what is being proposed..."

Rick Wakeman (Yes / Solo – Keyboards)

****

"The Plymouth Theater began its life in the 1930's. It is part of the history of cinema. It must be preserved for the future."

John Carpenter (Director – 'Halloween', 'The Thing', 'Escape From New York', 'They Live')

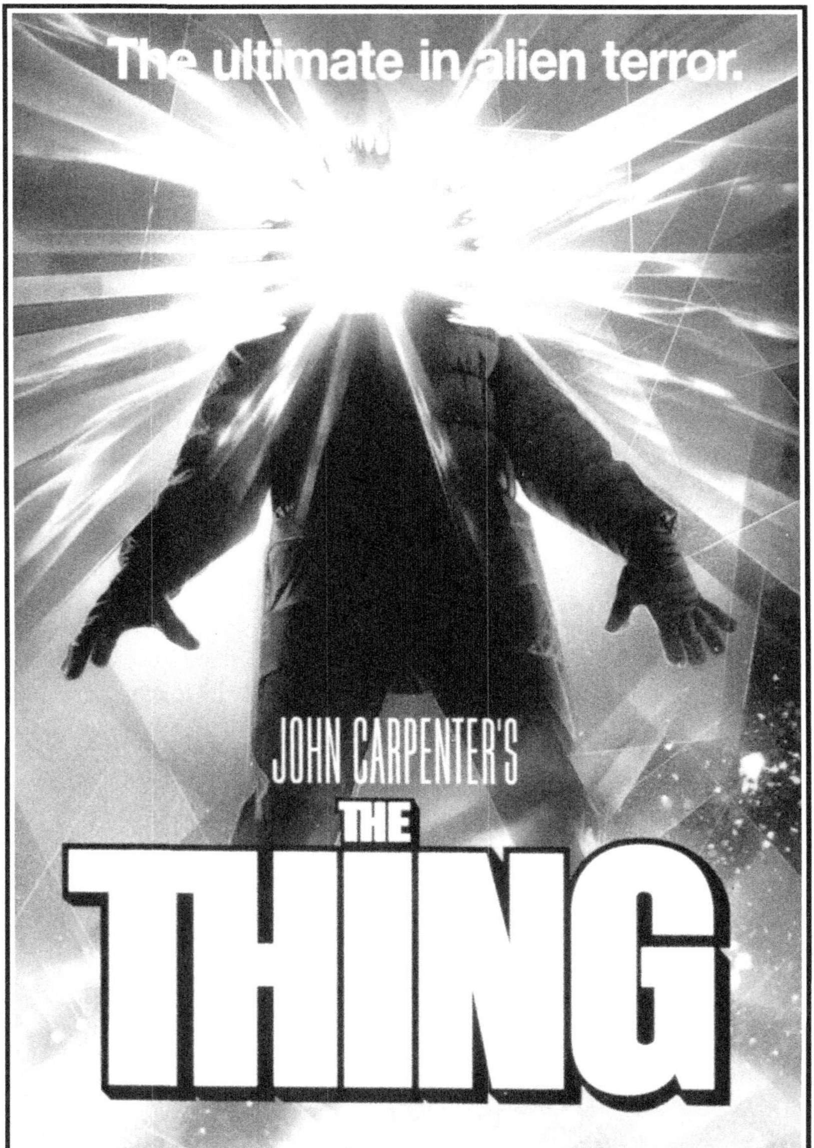
The ultimate in alien terror.
JOHN CARPENTER'S
THE
THING

"As a kid I remember going to the ABC, with ice creams at half time and in winter heaters on the walls.
A lovely old building in a city sadly full of concrete oblongs. As well as growing we also need to treasure the past and our heritage."

Sharron Davies (Olympic Swimmer & Sports Commentator)

****

"Always sad when a building that is part of the cultural history of a city is replaced by a developer's profit."

John Cleese
(Actor – Monty Python/Fawlty Towers)

****

"I am so sorry to hear of the threatened demolition of the ABC/REEL Cinema the only survivor from the golden Age of cinema when Plymouth boasted so many big screens and what we used to call 'flea pits'!
I remember seeing the Beatles□□□□□ there in '64, although too young. I think I queued all night pretending that I was staying with my cousin, who in turn was staying with me! I seem to remember the reports of the damp seats after the performance and I don't think it was Kia Ora!!!
During my time at Westward TV and TSW, we were regular visitors to the cinema and many happy lunches and after work drinks were taken in the bar next door way before it was 'Lorenzos', when it was still known as 'Sardis'.
Anyway it's another piece of Plymouth's history slipping away and one that students would appreciate I would have thought?"

Judi Spiers (TV and Radio Presenter)

****

"I spent many happy hours in the ABC cinema in the days of my youth in Plymouth.
My first courting was done there too and as the writer and poet, A. P. Herbert, expresses it well in three selected verses from a poem called -

'Twas at the Pictures, Child, We Met'.

No poet makes a special point
Of any human knee,
But in that plain prosaic joint
Was high romance for me.

Thus hand-in-hand and toe to toe,
Reel after reel we sat;
You are not old enough to know
The ecstasy of that.

And when the film was finished quite
It made my bosom swell
To find that by electric light
I loved her just as well.

This Art Deco cinema should be saved from demolition with a preservation order. A very good example is the one screen Rex cinema in Berkhamsted, a town of some 16,000 people. First opened in 1938, closed in 1988, it
re-opened in 2004 in its original style and has been a roaring success.
Good luck in trying to save it.

Lord David Owen
(Member of the House of Lords)

****

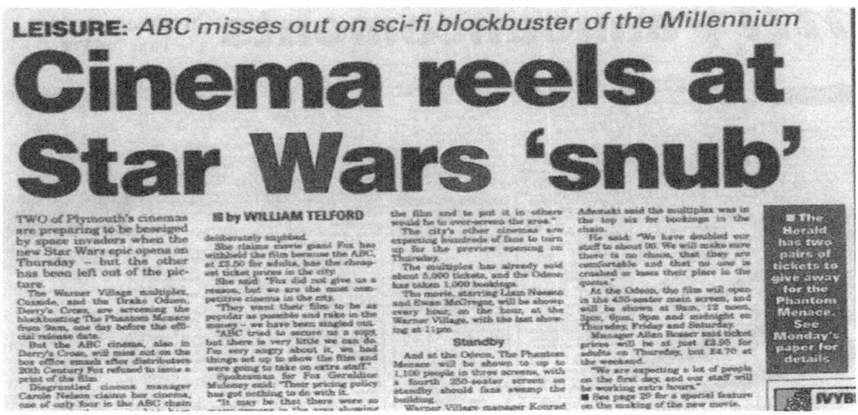

LEISURE: *ABC misses out on sci-fi blockbuster of the Millennium*

Cinema reels at Star Wars 'snub'

■ by WILLIAM TELFORD

TWO of Plymouth's cinemas are preparing to be besieged by space invaders when the new Star Wars epic opens on Thursday – but the other has been left out of the picture.

The Warner Village multiplex, Coxside, and the Drake Odeon, Derry's Cross, are screening the blockbusting The Phantom Menace from 9am, one day before the official release date.

But the ABC cinema, also in Derry's Cross, will miss out on the box office smash after distributors 20th Century Fox refused to issue a print of the film.

Disgruntled cinema manager Carole Nelson claims her cinema, one of only four in the ABC chain

deliberately snubbed.

She claims movie giant Fox has withheld the film because the ABC, at £3.50 for adults, has the cheapest ticket prices in the city.

She said: "Fox did not give us a reason, but we are the most competitive cinema in the city.

"They want their film to be as popular as possible and rake in the money – we have been singled out.

"ABC tried to secure us a copy, but there is very little we can do. I'm very angry about it, we had things set up to show the film and were going to take on extra staff."

Spokesman for Fox Geraldine Mulooney said: "Their pricing policy has got nothing to do with it.

"It may be that there were so

the film and to put it in others would be to over-screen the area."

The city's other cinemas are expecting hundreds of fans to turn up for the preview opening on Thursday.

The multiplex has already sold about 5,000 tickets, and the Odeon has taken 1,000 bookings.

The movie, starring Liam Neeson and Ewan McGregor, will be shown every hour, on the hour, at the Warner Village, with the last showing at 11pm.

Standby

And at the Odeon, The Phantom Menace will be shown to up to 1,100 people in three screens, with a fourth 250-seater screen on standby should fans swamp the building.

Warner Village manager Konrad Adamski said the multiplex was in the top six for bookings in the chain.

He said: "We have doubled our staff to about 90. We will make sure there is no chaos, that they are comfortable and that no one is crushed or loses their place in the queue."

At the Odeon, the film will open in the 450-seater main screen, and will be shown at 9am, 12 noon, 3pm, 6pm, 9pm and midnight on Thursday, Friday and Saturday.

Manager Allan Rosser said ticket prices will be at just £2.95 for adults on Thursday, but £4.70 at the weekend.

"We are expecting a lot of people on the first day, and our staff will be working extra hours."

■ See page 29 for a special feature on the making of the new movie.

■ The Herald has two pairs of tickets to give away for the Phantom Menace. See Monday's paper for details

Herald, Wednesday, Octob…

29

Faster than a game of Quidditch

TICKETS for the new Harry Potter movie are selling fast, say Plymouth cinema bosses.

Harry Potter and the Chamber of Secrets opens in the ABC and Warner Village cinemas in early November.

Warner Village ticket manager Alan Wilby said: "We've sold about 1,000 tickets so far – it looks as if the new film will do as well as the last."

Carole Nelson from ABC added: "Tickets have been selling like hotcakes. Judging by the interest, this will be biggest film of the year."

ON SALE: Vilma Damarell with movie tickets

Picture Claire Tregaskis

EA401830_CLT_002

BACK IN BUSINESS: (from left) Operations manager Muhammad Fa… manager Carole Nelson and Rebel Cinemas directors Ashley and Bar…

SCARLETT JOHANSSON

'A Rich History of Concerts'

"Did They Really Play Here?" Plymouth Rock, Metal & Punk Clubs & Gig Venues of the '70s to Now -

We have never had nationally 'well known' music venues in Plymouth like the Marquee or the 100 Club in London, Eric's or the Cavern in Liverpool, the Whisky-A-Go-Go, The Viper Rooms or the Roxy in Los Angeles or CBGB's in New York, but Plymouth has had (and still has) it's fair share of amazing venues and has hosted concerts by many worldwide renowned artists in our city.

Van Dike Club, Castaways, Metro, Woods, The Palace Theatre/Academy, Central Park, Speakeasy, Connexions, Ziggy's, Top Rank Suite, Abbey Hall, Poly, C103, White Rabbit, the Skating Rink, Fiesta, Cooperage, Plymouth Uni/Poly, Phoenix Tavern, Plymouth Guildhall, The Britannia, Ark Royal, Warehouse, Plymouth Pavilions, Voodoo Lounge, Home Park, Club Fandango, Volksfest, The Underground, The Junction, the Nowhere Inn, the Hippo/The Hub, Tiki Bar/Exile – so many venues, so many classic shows.

Who can say they were there to see Led Zeppelin at the Van Dike Club? the Sex Pistols 'Anarchy in the UK' tour at Woods? The Electric Light Orchestra at the Van Dike Club? KISS at the Plymouth Pavilions on the 'Revenge' tour? David Bowie at the Guildhall? Green Day on the

'American Idiot' tour at the Pavilions? Pink Floyd and Black Sabbath at the Van Dike Club? The Cure at the Metro, the Plymouth Polytechnic or Top Rank Suite? Roxy Music at the Van Dike Club? Whitesnake at Castaways? Supertramp at the Van Dike Club? Mott the Hoople at the Van Dike Club? So, many classic bands, so many wonderful memories.

But, one place that seems to have been forgotten about in regard to its use as a concert venue is the ABC/REEL Cinema.
People always seem to remember the Beatles playing there and no one else. But people also seem to have forgotten that the Beatles actually played there twice, once in 1963 and then again the following year as well. They were the most remembered, but the following list includes many of the other bands that graced the boards over the '60s and '70s.

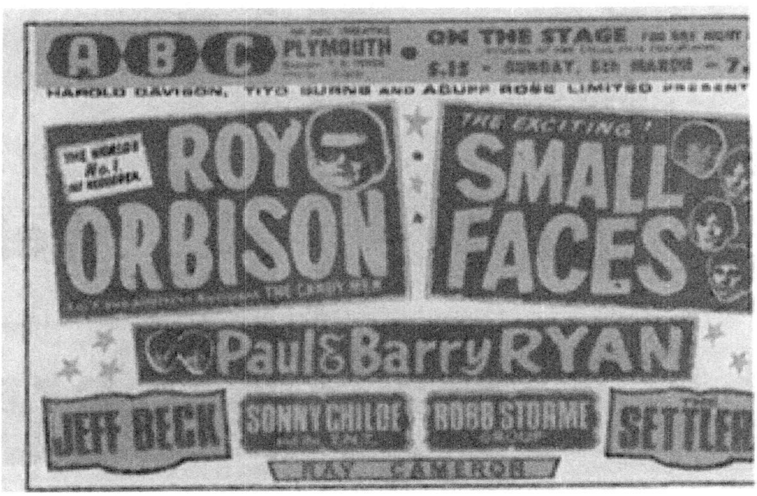

Some of the Concerts At the ABC/REEL Cinema

A Selection of the Concerts that the Cinema Has Held Over the Years:

7th May 1962 – **GARY 'U.S.' BONDS, JOHNNY BURNETTE**

22nd October 1962 - **BILLY FURY**

6th October 1963 - **BILLY FURY**

13th November 1963 – **THE BEATLES**

11th March 1964 – **GENE PITNEY**
BILLY J. KRAMER &
THE DAKOTAS
THE SWINGING BLUE JEANS

14th February 1964 – **GERRY AND THE PACEMAKERS**

8th April 1964 - **CLIFF RICHARD / SHADOWS**

19th May 1964 - **CHUCK BERRY,**
CARL PERKINS,
THE ANIMALS

29TH October 1964 - **THE BEATLES,**
MARY WELLS
TOMMY QUICKLY
THE REMO FOUR
SOUNDS INCORPORATED

27th April 1965 - **BILLY FURY**
BRIAN POOLE
AND THE TREMELOES
THE PRETTY THINGS

3rd November 1965 - **GENE PITNEY**
PETER & GORDON

4th December 1965 - **THE YARDBIRDS**
MANFRED MANN
THE SCAFFOLD

PAUL & BARRY RYAN
INEZ & CHARLIE FOXX
THE T-BONES
THE MARK LEEMAN FIVE

3rd November 1966 - **THE TROGGS**

5th March 1967 - **ROY ORBISON**
THE SMALL FACES
PAUL & BARRY RYAN
ROBB STORME THE WHISPERS

18th March 1967 - **THE WHO**

23rd November 1967 - **TOM JONES**

14th February 1971 - **DEEP PURPLE**

12th March 1971 - **EMERSON, LAKE & PALMER**

6th May 1971 - **CHUCK BERRY**

20th October 1971 - **T. REX**

27th November 1971 - **ELTON JOHN**

7th December 1975 - **JUSTIN HAYWARD**
& JOHN LODGE

16th December 1975 - **SUPERTRAMP**

3rd August 1976 - **ERIC CLAPTON**

****

Cinema drew an ABC of top stars

WHAT links the Beatles, the Rolling Stones and Cliff Richard and the Shadows?

The answer is that they all appeared on the stage of the ABC Cinema in Plymouth, as did other top names including the Everly Brothers, Chuck Berry, Roy Orbison, Lulu, Manfred Mann, the Animals, the Bee Gees, Tom Jones, Ken Dodd, the Small Faces, the Bay City Rollers, Olivia Newton John and Morecambe and Wise – not all at the same time, of course, but certainly all in the Sixties and Seventies, before the venue converted to a triple-screen-with-bingo affair in 1977.

Someone who was there to see it all, or at least most of it, is Paul Gregory – projectionist, technician and booth manager – who has worked behind the scenes at the ABC since 1967.

"The shame of it is," says Paul, "that we kept very little of the material that came with each concert – posters, flyers, programmes, photographs etcetera.

"Many of the things that did get preserved were only kept because someone had used the back of the poster or whatever to make notes or record information."

Although first and foremost a cinema throughout its almost-70-year history, the ABC – or the Royal, or the MGM Cannon, or the Odeon (as it is now) – has played host to some of the greatest names in the world of popular entertainment ... and even had the odd stage show here for a weekly run. Who remembers going to see the star of ITV's On The Buses, Bob Grant, appearing in The World's Longest-Running Permissive Sex Comedy, 'Pyjama Tops'?

Paul also has a few fascinating items of correspondence from Promoters, setting out their 'Stage and Theatre Requirements and Notes' for their artistes. Interestingly enough, both country star George Hamilton IV and Roger Whittaker required grand pianos, Roger's with the lid 'totally removed from the piano'. Mr Whittaker's requirements also included 'one bar stool on stage' ... 'THIS IS ESSENTIAL' said the notes in capital letters.

No great Spinal Tap-style stage props, lorryloads of gear and glitzy light shows in those days: just 'two follow spots with operators with selection of gel colours – red, blue, amber and pink ... together with any other available front and overhead lighting.'

The Bee Gees' gig on Friday, June 22, 1973, saw them arrive with a 15-piece orchestra, plus Alan Kendall on lead guitar and Dennis Byron (who had been with Amen Corner) on drums; the supporting act was Jimr Stevens.

It was a far cry from the crowd Sixties line-ups, when there would half a dozen or so acts on the sar bill, like the time 'the world's No.1 recorder' Roy Orbison came to tov with 'the exciting' Small Faces, Pa and Barry Ryan, Jeff Beck, the S tiers, Sonny Childe and the TNT, t Robb Storme group and R Cameron. And, yes: I lost the plot aft the Settlers too.

It was March 1967, Roy's curre single So Good, wasn't doing so go and neither was the Small Face single I Can't Make It, which was t first of five consecutive releases fro them not to make the top 10. The Pa and Barry Ryan single released coincide with the tour, Keep It Out Sight, was also destined to stay out the top 20.

Curiously enough, however, it w probably one of the few times that a rock guitarist Jeff Beck was happy play Hi-Ho Silver Lining. Releas that month, it was to be his first a biggest solo hit.

Tickets for the show ranged fro 15/- (75p) to a half of that, 7/6d, a there were two shows, one at 5.15p and the other at 7.45pm – how rock' roll was that?

You can drop Looking Back pictures and stories direct to Chris's Barbican studio at Chris Robinson Plymouth Prints, 34 New Street, Monday to Saturday. Readers can leave items with him, personally, most Wednesdays between 10am and 5pm.

"Saw my first concert at the ABC/REEL, 1971 - DEEP PURPLE and ASHTON, GARDENER and DYKE. 15/6p ticket (about 75p)!!"

Taff 'Rockin' Bear' Evans (Plymouth)

"Went to Eric Burden and the Animals, the Beatles and lots of films, just update it and keep our history."

Mary Dearing (Plymouth)

"I saw the Beatles too absolutely wonderful."

Sue Sparrow (Plymouth)

"I remember seeing lots of gigs at the old ABC Plymouth way back in the mid sixties when I was a schoolboy. In fact I was lucky enough to see so many bands/singers of the day there

that if you named one there's maybe a fifty per cent chance I'll have seen them, or at least that they'll have performed there.
But my first recollection of bands playing the ABC is actually about one I didn't see. My mate Jerry Skinner came into school one morning buzzing (I mean buzzing!) because he'd seen The Beatles there the night before, and I was – and still am - so envious. It was 1964 and mum said I was much too young to have gone.
'But mum! Jerry's allowed to go and he's four months younger than me...'
Move on to 1966. Mum at last relented and took me (I know – happy days!) to my first ever 'pop concert'. Five or six different top pop groups/artists of the day used to be packaged together at that time to tour the country, and Plymouth ABC was on the circuit for many of them. It was incredible value for money – all those acts for the price of one, and hence how I got to see so many.
There on stage were The Troggs, all wearing their signature white suits with the thick black stripe and purple roll neck jumpers – just like on Top of the Pops! Next up Dave Dee, Dozy, Beaky Mick and Tich, then perhaps a couple of lesser-known acts and finally – the Walker Brothers. Doubtless I'm completely muddled over which bands actually played that night, let alone in what order, but you'll get the gist.
For anyone who is old enough or sad enough to be interested, other acts I saw there over the following year or two include Herman's Hermits, Freddie and the Dreamers, PJ Proby, The Tremeloes, The Small Faces, Paul Jones, The Searchers, The Hollies (I think), Wayne Fontana and the Mindbenders, Pinkerton's Assorted Colours, Gene Pitney and the Spencer Davis Group.
One other artist that I feel deserves a special mention is Roy Orbison. Not even an act that I was really looking forward to – I didn't much care for ballads – but OMG what a voice!! I had never heard one so strong and rich – and it wasn't until I heard Paul Rodgers years later with Free at the Van Dike club that I heard another that even came close.

Speak as I find!
Roll forward many years, past Deep Purple, which I really enjoyed, to 1976 and I was delighted to get to see Eric Clapton for a second time.
That was until he staggered out on stage with a bottle of lager in one hand, clearly 'the worse for drink' as they say. In other words, he was well off his face.
Looking back it was at a time when he was having massive drink/addiction issues, so you have to sympathise with the guy.
Anyway, EC is EC and he got away with rattling out a load of mainly twelve bars; I've always been a massive Clapton fan and I loved it!"

Pete Phillips (Plymouth)

Eric Clapton
ABC Cinema, Plymouth
'No Reason to Cry' Tour
3rd August 1976

All Our Past Times
Farther Up the Road
Tell the Truth
Ramblin' on My Mind
Have You Ever Loved a Woman
Call It Stormy Monday (But Tuesday Is Just as Bad)
Hungry
Knockin' on Heaven's Door
Innocent Times
Blues Power

"Back in the '50s when I was still at school, Tommy Steele was there and my friend Pat Hughes & I got T-shirts and embroidered his name on the front of them, as no print service back then. Seen my Cliff with his Shadows there & Tom Jones with knickers being thrown. Ha!
Oh I remember seeing the Beatles too. I went with my sister & we were sat upstairs in the back row and they were so tiny from there like real beetles, everyone was screaming and so were we. Hardly heard a thing. Ha ha!"

Teresa Crook (Plymouth)

"Saw the New Seekers at ABC - 21st April 1972.
Went out looking for them following the show - found them inside the Duke of Cornwall Hotel, by which time my parents had called the police as I was not home by 4.00am the following morning, lol."

Jill Burgess (Plymouth)

"I saw T. Rex live at the ABC with my friends in 1971 - very exciting as girls were fainting all over the place and had to be carried out by St John's Ambulance!
Saw country legend George Hamilton IV there in 1975 - great live music and big acts performed there - great memories of this wonderful building."

Sally Ann West (Plymouth)

"I saw the Beatles there in 1964 and I was 16 and I went with a group of friends, I screamed my head off!
We didn't hear a word they sang, as we screamed the whole way through it."

Julie Bell (Plymouth)

The Beatles
ABC Cinema, Plymouth
29th October 1964

Twist and Shout
Money (That's What I Want)
Can't Buy Me Love
Tings We Said Today
I'm Happy Just to Dance With You
I Should Have Known Better
If I Fell
I Wanna Be Your Man
A Hard Day's Night
Long Tall Sally

"I saw the Beatles, the Rolling Stones and Deep Purple here back in the day."

Sheila Crews (Plymouth)

"I had a 'pavement sleep' there, in order to get tickets for the Beatles."

Felicity Barrett (Plymouth)

"I saw many live shows including David Whitfield, Ruby Murray, Peters and Lee."

Leslie Parsons (Plymouth)

"My mum took me and my friend to see the Beatles. My friend and I couldn't speak for a week afterward due to us screaming constantly. The Auditorium was packed."

Pat McGrew (Plymouth)

"I saw Cliff and the Shadows for the first time here back in 1964."

Pat Branson (Plymouth)

Cliff Richard & The Shadows
ABC Cinema, Plymouth
8th April 1964

Whole Lotta Shakin' Goin On
Twenty Four Hours From Tulsa
Da Doo Ron Ron
It's All in the Game
You Don't Know
Constantly
The Young Ones
Don't Talk to Him
Bachelor Boy
What'd I Say

"I remember back in the '60s going to the ABC to see The Walker Brothers. The line up was fantastic with Dave Dee, Dozy, Beaky, Mick and Tich - Paul and Barry Ryan - The Troggs and many more supporting acts.
I'll never forget that night."

Gillian Sargent (Plymouth)

"In the sixties I saw Cliff & the Shadows, Gene Pitney, Herman's Hermits, the Troggs and many others - good memories."

Marg Leycock (Melksham)

"I saw The Beatles here in 1963 and many other stars of the day."

Linda Davidson (Saltash, Cornwall)

The Beatles
ABC Cinema, Plymouth
13th November 1963

I Saw Her Standing There
From Me to You
All My Loving
You've Really Got a Hold on Me
Roll Over Beethoven
Boys
Till There Was You
She Loves You
Money (That's What I Want)
Twist and Shout

"I saw the Bay City Rollers there in the mid '70s. Couldn't hear a thing except for the screaming."

Liz Walch (Plymouth)

"I have two stories relating to the ABC in Plymouth
First: 1963
The Beatles played the ABC in 1963 and although only 2 years old my mum took me along to this concert along with some old people from the Thorn Park Nursing home that she was matron of in Manamead.

Quite how I was allowed in at that young age I can't even begin to imagine but we must remember this was the 1960's!
Obviously I have no real recollection of this concert except that we were on a balcony away from the young fans and my overwhelming memory is of peering over the edge and hearing the most incredible din that was screaming.
My mum loved her music and I'm sure that this early experience for me lit the fuse for what was to become a lifelong passion for live concerts.

Second: 1974

It's the 1970's and the Bay City Rollers are at the peak of their fame and I got to meet them after their ABC gig.
It's a mid-week gig and from lunchtime let's say an awful lot of Plymouth schoolgirls haven't turned up for afternoon classes. No, they're all on the Royal Parade which has turned into a fast moving river of tartan and ridiculously high platform shoes as they – me included – made their way down to queue outside the ABC.
Okay, the show isn't starting until 7.30pm but that doesn't matter, it's all about the camaraderie you see, fans together, singing, chanting, whipping each other up into a frenzy.
I didn't like the group at all. I was there under duress and I'll tell you why.
My school friend Carolyn and I had an agreement, we liked opposite types of music, I'd accompany her if she accompanied me, and so in exchange for her seeing 10.CC with me the year before it was my turn. And I entered into the spirit of the occasion with tartan scarves tied to my wrists, which was another part of the Rollers get up.
Once inside I genuinely have no real recollection of the concert other than there being intense screaming and bodies flying all over the place as girls clamoured over seats and down aisles to get as near to the stage as possible.
But I do have a clear memory of what happened afterwards. As hordes of fans ran up towards the Holiday Inn - where the group was staying -Carolyn was devastated that she couldn't go too but her dad had insisted on picking us up outside in his car.

What neither of us knew was that instead of going straight home we were driven round the back of the Holiday Inn to the underground car park, ushered into the lift and taken to one of the upper floors, neither of us spoke, just looked at each other, what the hell was going on?!
Her dad was 'something in entertainment' and clearly had good contacts. So there we were, being led into this big room filled with a large gaggle of people and the lads from the Rollers were lined up having their hands shook, we were only 13 years old so were totally in awe of everything around us.
The boys – because they were still boys – looked shattered, very hot and sweaty, we too got to shake their hands, Carolyn managed to stay upright without fainting, we got autographs, her dad took a group photo of us with them; we thanked them, she told them they were wonderful and walked out towards the lift!"

Ellie Hudson (Plymouth)

Emerson, Lake & Palmer
ABC Cinema, Plymouth
12th March 1971

The Barbarian
Tarkus
Knife-Edge
Pictures at an Exhibition
Take a Pebble (fugue)
Ballad of Blue
Take a Pebble (fugue)
Blue Rondo a la Turk
Nutrocker

"My memory of the Bay City Rollers was of hysterical stupid screaming girls and not being able to hear the music!!! As bad as it probably was!"

Yvonne Lovering (Plymouth, UK)

"In I think about 1974 The Bay City Rollers played there I was mad on them, but my mother wouldn't let me go. I was 11. She did however make my sister and her boyfriend go (they were about 17) and delighted NOT to have to go.
They were sent to get me some memorabilia and dutifully got me a programme, scarf (tartan of course) and strangely some white nylon socks with their image on the side.
Well the first time I wore them my dad helped with the washing. You boiled your 'whites' in a Baby Burco Boiler, yep you guessed the pictures came off completely.
I cried for days and dad was never allowed to forget it."

Christine Ewings (Plymouth)

*"**Lemanis**" at Reel Cinema*

It was February 22nd, 2009
It was in screen 2, which is part of the main stage in the 60's the Beatles played on, but most of that stage is in the Bingo hall now.
I remember it being talked about in the paper and on the radio as "The first gig since the Beatles" but have heard that a couple

of times since when other acts have played, and there were probably a few before us. It sounds good though.
We were supported by our friends Head of Programmes and on that day we were 11 piece, I think.
There was a lot of excitement for it and there was a good crowd. At the end we didn't want it to end and the audience didn't seem to want it to.
We ran out of songs and I remember walking round the band during the applause telling everyone the chords to one more, which we did at the end. But we didn't know how to end it of course as we hadn't practiced, so I just walked off and left the band to deal with it, which they did expertly.
Amazing memories of that day!"

Chris Muirhead(Plymouth)

"I am not sure if you are aware of us at Casa, but not too long ago we held a very successful music event in the Reel Cinema, which was very financially rewarding for both ourselves - but mainly the theatre.
We are very much behind saving this historic building and anything we can do to help, you have our full support. We hoped that our previous efforts could build awareness and show the value of saving this wonderful space for events such as ours.

Ben Gill-Carey (Casa Events)

'Saturday Morning Pictures'

"Loved Sat Morning pictures, also a lovely Building.
Saturday morning pictures, 'Flash Gordon'.
Brings back so many good memories over the years when it was the ABC – Iconic building."

Sheila Bentley (Plymouth)

"It was usually something like 'The Double Deckers', a few cartoons and then a film from the 'Childrens Film Foundation'. We all stood up for the 'National Anthem' at the start and sometimes there was a sing-along."

Liz Walch (Plymouth)

"Saturday morning pictures!!"

Candy Hoskins (Exeter)

"I too used to go to Saturday mornings, with my brother and cousin then go and get chips and scraps – the batter bits with plenty of vinegar.
The chip shop stood between King Street and Union Street, where
Toys R Us is now.
The highlight of Saturday.
If it was a 'Cowboy and Indians' film, we would pretend we were them, hiding behind walls."

Jean Holt (Plymouth)

"I remember going to Saturday morning in the fifties.

Marg Leycock (Melksham)

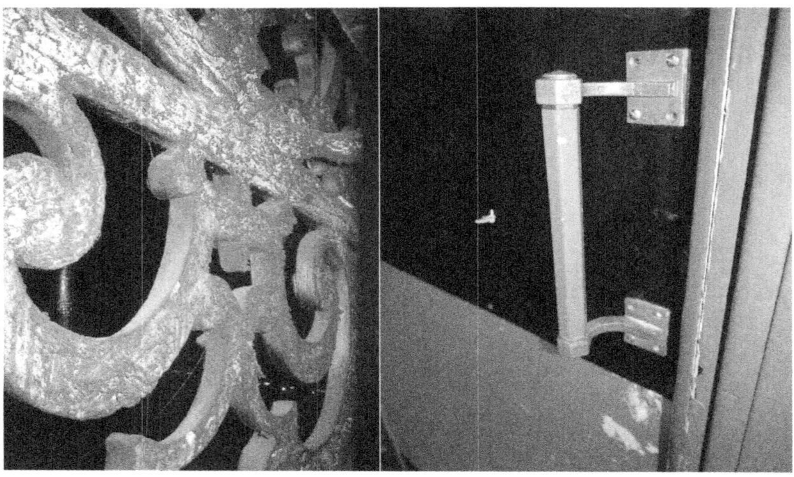

"Started going Saturday morning pictures when I was 7 back in 1951. All by myself.
Always tried to sit in the same seat. It was 6d to go in and 3d for an ice-lolly.
The organ used to come up, being played by a famous local organist (he used to be on the radio). The organ used to change

colours. There was a sing-song with the words on screen.
Then a cartoon, the serial 'Captain Marvel' or 'Flash Gordon', maybe an educational type film.
Then an interval.
The main feature could be anything from 'Laurel & Hardy', 'Bud Abbott & Lou Costello' to a cowboy such as 'Roy Rogers', or even a swashbuckling adventure film.
We had our 6d worth back then. Oh, and if we attended regularly we got ABC badges presented on stage!"

Susan Cotter (Plymouth)

"The good thing about 'Saturday Morning Pictures', is you would always get entertained before a showing especially for me seeing magic by magician Pip Critten.
Oh what joy!"

Tristan Michael Tozer (Plympton)

"As a young lad of 9 years, I old spent many a Saturday morning with my mates at the 'Saturday Morning Pictures'. Seem to remember they had guest performances of a strong man trying to bend six-inch nails etc. before the film started.
Good times had by all.
One of the most remembered parts of growing up."

Gaz Landricombe (Plymouth)

"There's a collage in the men's loo's, which includes a pic of a queue for the Saturday morning shows.
On the corner wall, between the urinals... hilarious!"

Cherrie Harvey (Plymouth)

"I used to go every Saturday morning, as a child. The lady on the till got to recognize me and used to speak to me when I went as an adult."

Pat McGrew (Plymouth)

"As a kid I loved going to the Saturday morning picture show. My mum would go shopping and I'd sit and get lost in films and cartoons for a few hours. It was a good deal for the both of us. My mum could shop in peace and I didn't have to be 'dragged' around food and clothing stores.
My preference to going to the ABC rather than Drakes Cinema was due to the ABC having special guests and a better atmosphere. I remember some lady from 'Crossroads', a cartoonist called 'Scribble' from ITV and animals from Sparkwell Zoo (now Dartmoor Zoological Park)."

Andy Gillies (Plymouth)

"Saturday morning pictures 'Famous Five' and 'St Trinians' such good memories."

Sharon Davis (Plympton)

"I remember going to the 'kids am' with my friends that was fun."

Claire McLatchie (Plymouth)

"Remember going to Saturday morning pictures here with my brother."

Maureen Hocking (Plymouth)

"Remember my dad dropping me there to meet friends to watch Saturday morning pictures. Loved dancing at the front before the movie started. Also had my first stolen kiss in there.
Sweet memories x"

Sarah Rogers (Plymouth)

"Saturday morning pictures with a couple of school mates, my mum used to give me a bag of sweets to take with me."

P.A.Smith (Slochteren, Netherlands)

"Went to many Saturday morning picture shows too!
Peter Cushing as 'Doctor Who' etc."

Ian Randell (Exeter)

"I spent half my youth in that wonderful cinema. From the Saturday morning kids club at 50p a ticket, to various teenage dates."

Gay Chester (Prestwich)

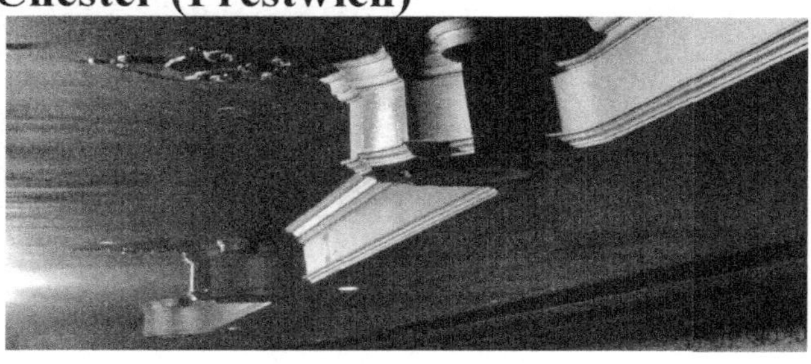

'Ghostly Encounters'

"Back two/three years ago in March/April I went to the ABC/REEL Cinema to watch 'Spider-Man'.
I went with a family friend and she needed the toilet but wanted me to walk down with her and wait (we were watching in the main/biggest screen) as I waited outside I felt a massive tightening to my right thigh as if someone was really, really gripping on and wrapping something or their arms/hands around me, it was so, so tight.
I began to panic and I couldn't shake it off it took a good few minutes before it finally was released and I was so close to tears as I had never experienced anything up until then. It's only the proper real thing I've ever experienced - as in touch wise - but I am quite scared of paranormal things. I am quite in tune with

ghosts/spirits and can usually feel a presence, although there is a certain screen (Screen 2) where I feel like I'm being stared at by someone in one of the seats towards the back and occasionally front of the screen.
I've not been in so long as people refuse to go with me and after mentioning the story to my mum, she refuses to go with me as well."

Shan Gessey (Plymouth)

"I was touched on the shoulder when we had OAP club in Screen 2, when I looked up at the projection hole."

Duncan Jago (Plymouth)

"I went to the Reel Cinema for a haunted night lock down with the 'Haunted Apparitions' team - which I do a lot - but I must say that the experience I had in the Reel Cinema nothing has come close.
I have been going ghost hunting for many years with the 'Haunted Apparitions' team and my best ever experience was in the Reel Cinema.
I always go here and not long ago was ghost hunting and that's where I saw my first ghost.
Here is my story, on the night, of the haunted night, I was so excited got ready with my husband, lots to drink and food to keep us going through the night.
Through the night we did all the things we normally do in the group with the glass etc.
Then we had a break which was in the big cinema, I was sat in the front row maybe 7th row to the left and I saw a man figure in uniform I couldn't believe it was amazing a girl about 7 chairs across said the same thing so I new I wasn't seeing things it was one of the best experiences of my life."

Andrea Ward (Plymouth)

"A few members of staff did a lock in, a couple of seats sounded like fingernails were being dragged along them. Four loud bangs on the Screen 2 door and something touched the back of my neck."

Paul Smith (Plymouth)

"Also I've been there for a ghost hunt; that was amazing."
Paula Moran (Plymouth)

"I've also led a paranormal investigation of the Cinema as Chairman of 'Haunted Devon' on 2 occasions. We mainly focused on Screen 2, again - as this is the most active according to staff reports. The moment when I'm sat on my own in the dark and one of the seats returns to the 'upright' position is one I'll never forget. I'm a big lad but my legs did 'wobble' a bit! We never did see the infamous 'Grey lady' but we did have a few strange experiences."
Andy Gillies (Plymouth)

"I attended a paranormal investigation there a few years ago and to say I was genuinely shaken would be an understatement. The famously haunted area - the ladies' loo's - yielded nothing for our group, neither did the main screen.
However, the claustrophobic screen 3 was a different ballgame altogether.
About 5 of us scattered around, I was sat on left hand side of the aisle about halfway back. I had the EMF meter and to begin

with, it did nothing at all. Within a few minutes, it started flashing and beeping on and off, and I couldn't move. I was also freezing cold - everyone else was sweating, it was so warm in there.

The leader of the group then asked whatever spirit was in the room to walk towards the front of the room and the EMF meter petered out. He asked it to walk to the back and the meter started beeping and flashing again, fading off.

This was tried several times, with the same result each time. There were also black orbs caught on the nightvision camera, moving quickly when the 'spirit' was asked to move across the room.

A truly terrifying experience.

Kay Scoble (Plymouth)

Whispers hint at cinema haunting

CINEMA VIGIL: Front, from left, Alan Baugh, Goldy Bromley, and back, John Irons, Denise O'Driscoll and Terry Bowen

A GHOST investigation team from London has witnessed some spooky goings-on at Plymouth's Reel Cinema.

Goldy's Ghosts – the self-proclaimed 'most popular ghost-hunting team in the UK' – was invited down to Plymouth to check out the former ABC Cinema.

Goldy Bromley, who leads the group, said she was in no doubt that the cinema near Derry's Cross was haunted by 'some form of phenomena'.

Her team caught ghostly whispers on tape, footsteps on video and the CCTV cameras at the cinema mysteriously cut out during the investigation.

Goldy brought with her two of her most trusted mediums – John Irons and Terry Bowen – to make contact with spirits in the cinema.

She also brought down a ghost-hunting crew, and staff at the cinema helped out.

The mediums said they had made contact with several spirit energies in the cinema. Names which they noted included Annette Dilberry, Lily Putt, William Penrose and an eight-year-old boy called Jack.

An EVP (Electronic Voice Phenomena) machine, which records sound, was set up in the cinema throughout the investigation. The group claims the name 'Maggie' can be heard in spooky whispers.

The words 'ABC' were also heard being spoken in a woman's voice – even though the team had no idea the building was once the ABC Cinema.

Other strange goings-on included footsteps being heard and caught on video, and the vision of a woman dressed in white.

Burning was also smelled by a few of the ghost-hunters and a mass of 'cold energy' reportedly appeared in front of one of the screens.

There was also some movement behind one of the closed doors in the cinema which was witnessed by all the team and staff members – but no rational explanation could be found.

Goldy said: "It was an eventful investigation which brings me to only one conclusion – that the Reel Cinema is nicely haunted."

Goldy's group has been established for more than nine years and she is a psychic trance medium.

For more details on the group, log on to the website www.goldysghosts.co.uk

'Around the Building'

REEL
REEL CINEMA

'Final Curtain'

So, there we have it – the people have spoken.

We have campaigned and had many meetings –over many months - to save the building, but it's future is now in ***your*** hands. Write to your local MP, contact the City Council, badger your next door neighbours to join in and support our/your efforts by buying this book and helping fight the cause*.

From all of the comments that I have received over the past year for this book, you all feel the same as we do – that the building ***should live on***, providing a community cinema / 1000 capacity music venue / art space etc.

It would be extremely sad to see the building go, so many memories, so many concerts, so many films, so much popcorn!!

We leave the ball in your court.
Support us, help us and promote the campaign to help save '***our Last Picture House***'.

Ian Carroll
21st June 2018

*50% of Book sales will be going towards producing leaflets, stationary, promotional items – none will be squandered on popcorn...

Don't lower a final curtain

AST Saturday
night, having
failed to find any-
thing worth
hing on television
ite having 488
nels to choose from
days), the man in
ife and I decided to
are out of the house
change, and go to
inema.
en the sad state of our
at present (no cash to
of, and fast approaching
ge where they laugh at
nightclubs), the cinema
red to be our best

wasted an hour or so on
evitable debate about
to Watch, running
h the usual gender
types – he demanded
hing involving sub-
es/nuclear warheads or
nd I sang the praises of
se cinema, or at least
ng with Brad Pitt in it.
ntually we gave up and
tickets for a newly-
d high-octane, sci-fi
uster.
man in my life was
because people were
to be brutally beaten up by
ddies, and I was satisfied
e at least there wouldn't be
bmarines in it.
we went, arriving in good
stock up on the obligatory
n and ice cream.
had great seats and there
body in front of us, so we
lop our legs over the next
d stretch out in comfort.
film was fine, as these
go, and provided a few
of distracting and fairly
g escapist fluff (admittedly
Pitt, but the guy with the
laws wasn't bad).
ny overwhelming memory
evening wasn't of the
ive special effects or the
ast, and it wasn't even of
orn, tasty as it was.
left wondering why the
had been less than a quar-

dn't go to the Warner Vil-
nema at the Barbican
Park, you see. If we had, I
the cinema would have
ked; this was a brand-new
a series with a fairly
blished cult following
starring a host of household names.

The Warner Village multiplex was no doubt booked up that Saturday night with hundreds of people streaming in to watch the movie at all of the numerous time slots it was on offer.

But, as I said, we didn't go there: we went to the tiny little ABC Cinema at Derry's Cross, and there can't have been more than 75 people sharing the 580-seat theatre with us.

I have absolutely no idea why, and it's been puzzling me all week.

The ABC Cinema is a fantastic place; it's crammed with wonderful features and examples of 1930s interior design, from the plush red velour chairs to the elaborate corniced ceiling.

There is even a pleated red satin curtain which rises dramatically before the film begins.

Ticket prices are incredibly good value for money at the ABC, and the staff make quite possibly the best popcorn in the world.

On top of all this, you now can park for free right next door in the Theatre Royal car park, and there are some lovely pubs, bars and restaurants yards away to choose from, including the ever-popular Lorenzo's and Pizza Express.

But every time I visit the ABC Cinema it's never packed, it's never usually more than half-full, and it worries me.

Not because I want to be squashed in at the end of the front row craning my neck to see the screen, as all the seats are taken: of course it's nice to have the place to yourself and the pick of the seats, but because I don't want to see the ABC close down from a lack of business.

Thankfully, the ABC is not under any threat of closure at the moment; the advent of the Warner Village multiplex and increased parking charges may have rung the death-knell of the neighbouring Drake Odeon in 1999, but the ABC Cinema has so far managed to stay afloat.

Manager Carole Nelson tells me that while the Warner Village has affected business, they're doing OK at the moment, and points out that this time of year is never a very busy time for cinemas.

I'm delighted to know my favourite cinema isn't about to be knocked down and turned into yet another nightclub, but I'd feel a lot happier if more people were using it to ensure it never will be.

Don't get me wrong; I'm not urging you to steer clear of the Warner Village, and neither am I criticising it in any way.

I like the Warner Village multiplex very much: it's a fabulous place with dozens of cinema screens, excellent sound quality and extremely comfy bucket seats which have nifty little built-in cup holders for your popcorn and drinks.

It is also a huge multiplex able to show every film currently on general release at regularly spaced intervals.

But what it doesn't have is a history, and the character that inevitably comes with that.

The ABC Cinema may be much smaller, it may only offer a small selection of movies and the seats may not have cup holders, but it is a wonderful old-style cinema with bags of character and a fantastic atmosphere. It's also cheap, cosy, friendly – and did I mention how nice the popcorn is?

Popcorn aside, I don't see why Plymouth can't have both: there's no doubt we need a big cinema like the Warner Village to cater for a city this size, but surely that doesn't mean we can't use our lovely old ABC as well?

Over the years, we have seen the loss of the village post office and the local branch of the high-street bank, while every time a new supermarket opens it poses a threat to a little corner shop.

I have never understood why bringing in the new also has to mean chucking out the old. Why can't we enjoy both – stock up at the supermarket and still make use of the corner shop when we run out of milk?

The same applies to our cinemas: the Warner Village is very often packed to bursting when I visit and the ABC isn't, so if you're planning to see a film, why not visit the ABC now and again and give it a turn?

There are surely enough cinema-goers in Plymouth to make good use of both these facilities, and ensure that we never risk losing either of them.

Other Books Available
By Ian Carroll

Music Books

The Reading Festival: Music, Mud and Mayhem

From Donington to Download

Lemmy: Memories of a Rock 'N' Roll Legend –

Welcome to Cornwall Coliseum

From Flint With Blood – A Short History of King 810

Ronnie James Dio: The Man on the Silver Mountain

Leonard Cohen: Just One More Hallelujah

The Fans Have Their Say #1 KISS – We Wanted the Best and We Got the Best

The Fans Have Their Say #2 AC/DC – Rock 'n' Roll From the Land Down Under

The Fans Have Their Say #3 – Black Sabbath – The Lords of Darkness

The Fans Have Their Say #4 – Guns N' Roses – Welcome to the Jungle

Horror Books

The Lovers Guide To Internet Dating

Demon Pirates Vs Vikings

Valentines Day

My Name Is Ishmael

A-Z of Bloody Horror 'A' is for 'Antique Shop'

A-Z of Bloody Horror 'C' is for 'Clown in Aisle 3'

A-Z of Bloody Horror 'M' is for 'Warning: Water May Contain Mermaids'

A-Z of Bloody Horror 'P' is for 'Pensioner'

on Kindle and in Paperback

Projectionist Paul's had the
same job since he left school

After 11th-hour rescue, owner says:

'I COULDN'T LET REEL DIE'

THE new operator of Plymouth's Reel Cinema says he has come out of retirement because he didn't want to see the building close.

by DOMINIC JEFF
Herald Reporter

Barry Willis, 69, said his company, Rebel Cinemas, had sold its last property and closed its bank account, but when he read about the Reel closing he knew he had to move fast to save it.

"I just don't like to see something like this snuffed out," he said.

"There are going to be difficult times but there's a lot of history in a building like this. It might only be a shadow of what it once was but millions of people have been through the doors in the last 70 years."

He said he was passionate about cinema and had definitely not taken over the Reel for business reasons.

Until a couple of weeks ago Mr Willis had been enjoying his retirement. Then he read about the imminent closure of the cinema in a trade magazine and decided to act.

The cinema had been due to close on Thursday, and he started negotiations with Reel about 10 days before but nothing was made public until the deal was signed, on the day which was earmarked for its closure.

New Rebel Cinemas will run the cinema and Reel will continue to own the building. There had been fears that the old cinema would be demolished to make way for a new multiplex.

Yesterday Mr Willis visited the Reel for the hand-over, and told The Herald: "My opinion was that if it had closed last night the doors would never have opened again, especially with the economic downturn."

The 11-hour deal means the cinema will not close at all; when negotiations started, Reel took the precaution of booking films for next week.

Last month, The Herald revealed the construction firm which owned the Reel chain was in talks about replacing the 1938 picture-house at Derry's Cross with a '21st-century' development.

Loughborough-based 3R Construction and Property Development owns the 16-cinema Reel chain, and managing director Kailesh Suri told The Herald last month: "We will be developing and will have a new cinema on it.

"It depends on planning permission. We're in the consultation stage."

It also emerged that developers had been eyeing the neighbouring Athenaeum, possibly as part of the cinema development.

The Reel, formerly the ABC, is the city's only survivor from the golden age of pictures when Plymouth boasted numerous big screens and fleapits. The Beatles famously played there in the 1960s.

Rebel Cinemas, a family firm, ran the Rebel Cinema near Bude in North Co
wall until last year. Before that,
Willis ran a three-screen cinema
Shropshire for 25 years.

He said he had not had time to m
plans for his new operation, althoug
would continue to show mainstre
commercial films.

He could not comment on the lo
term future of the 17 staff at the R
who this week were delighted to h
the cinema had been saved. "Obvious
have to look for savings," he said.

Under the licence agreement, Re
would have to seek Reel's permission
make physical changes to the buildi

However, Mr Willis said he was
thinking of that yet, but just conc
trating on keeping the cinema going

Mr Willis appealed for people in P
mouth to go and use the cinema, say
it needed the support of local custom
if it was to be a success.

He intended to keep the Reel na
because the cinema had had too ma
name changes in the past, he added.

■ Pending a link being reopened
Reel cinema's web page, there
currently nowhere to find film times
the Reel Cinema.

Customers are advised that the b
thing is to just go along. Films show
next week will be How to Lose Frie
and Alienate People, Disaster Mov
Death Race, Space Chimps, Tropic Thunder and Taken.

Printed in Great Britain
by Amazon

36519386R00079